A VAGABOND IN NEW YORK

My favorite pitch is the ring of benches round the fountain opposite the General Post Office.

A VAGABOND IN NEW YORK

BY

OLIVER MADOX HUEFFER

Author of "The Artistic Temperament," "Hunt the Slipper," "Where Truth Lies," etc., etc.

EIGHT ILLUSTRATIONS

BY

ROY E. HALLINGS

NEW YORK: JOHN LANE COMPANY
LONDON: JOHN LANE, THE BODLEY HEAD
TORONTO: BELL & COCKBURN MCMXIII

THE VAIL-BALLOU COMPANY
Binghamton, New York, U. S. A.

"EHRWARTEND"

"For to admire and for to see,
  For to be'old this world so wide;
It never done no good to me,
  But I can't stop it if I tried."

Kipling.

PREFACE

AT the time when some of these sketches were appearing in the pages of *Truth* I received a letter from an earnest-minded reader, enquiring whether they were supposed to be "remotely founded on fact," or were merely "the imaginative efforts of a common or garden liar." Perhaps I should therefore preface them in their collected form with the assurance that they are one and all "founded on fact," not over and above remotely. They are based, as they profess to be, upon the experiences of a young Englishman during a period of vagabondage enjoyed in New York and thereabouts. They do not however claim the exact fidelity to fact of Hansard or a Law Report. Vagabondage is a mental no less than a physical state of being and, just as a tramp's progress across the sunny side of life is less direct than is, say, that of a bank-manager through the shadows, so his mind recalls less faithfully all and every entry in the mnemonical ledger. Perhaps then, in this narrative some terminological inexactitude may here and there find expression in word, or exclamation mark, or period. Here and there memory may heighten a high-light or erase a shadow. No vagabond could be expected to swear in a court of law to the exact size or brilliancy of every politician's near-diamond bosom-pin which may have cast its light across his path — or his pages — or that the politician smoked exactly such a cigar as memory recalls, or indeed that he smoked a cigar at all. Sufficient, surely, that as such the Vagabond recalls him, as smoking, and smoking a cigar, and that the cigar was very large and rank. Be it at least believed by the gentlemen of the jury that such a politician there was, such a steamboat skipper, such a policeman, such an elephant, as those the Vagabond has sought to draw, and that their doings and sayings, their relationship towards him and towards each other are recorded with as much fidelity as memory will allow.

Naturally again, they do not appear under their real names. You may walk miles along Sixth Avenue and never find Mr. Cholmondely's laboratory; the Officer who directs the traffic at the corner of Broadway and Union Square will not answer to the name of Dempsey; may even deny the existence of any officer answering to that name. Yet you may believe without fear of being led astray that Mr. Cholmondely, however called, is at this moment somewhere adapting chickens to a new career; that Dempsey, whitest man who ever trod shoe-leather, is somewhere directing traffic; that somewhere Gladys, unmindful of her earlier loves, is making eyes — red, piggy eyes — at her mahout of the moment.

Let it not be thought that these poor sketches make any claim to pass as "Impressions of America" or that they profess to picture New York, or any aspect of it, or anything at all but the little piece of sidewalk upon which the Vagabond's eyes have fallen as he quartered it in search of cigarette-ends. His not the conquering brain, the all-seeing eye, that can compress a nation within the limits of a single volume, as do those Kings of English Literature who from time to time make Royal Progresses across the Atlantic and back for Literary purposes. No fatted calves were ever slain for the Prodigal Vagabond; no streets were ever decorated; no Fifth Avenue mansions flung open against his coming. He has but hung upon the skirts of the cheering crowd, thankful if, from afar off, he might catch some vague glimpse of the Features, the Repose, of the Great Man. Not for him to be dined and wined, to be fêted and ovated; to discuss, while thousands hang enraptured on his lips or weep over the whorlings of his fruitful pen, the Spirit of the American People, the Tendencies of American Social Life, the Prospects of American Literature, or, most precious of all, Himself and his Undying Works, considered in the light of American royalties. No one realises more fully than does the shabby Vagabond the impertinence that bids him cry, even in the smallest of voices, these Gutter Gleanings. At least let it be remembered in his favour that he does fully realise his own limitations; that he is well aware that his vision is from Below, not from Above. He would plead also that if his point of view be petty and sordid, and with no wish or claim to be Literary, it is at least sincere.

I have to express my thanks to the the editor of *Truth* for his courteous permission to include among the rest certain sketches which originally appeared in that journal.

O. M. H.

CONTENTS

ILLUSTRATIONS

A VAGABOND IN NEW YORK

CHAPTER I

A Baby in the Bronx

I AM not, fundamentally, a baby-worshipper. Though, admittedly, necessary to our present stage of evolution, they have always seemed to me to be adorable rather in the abstract than in the concrete and, although I hope that, in a case of shipwreck, I should willingly give up my place in the boats to all or any babies who might be involved, I am not altogether sure that my motive would be one of pure chivalry. Better death, I am inclined to think, than, say, six babies within a radius of twenty feet.

Nevertheless, there are babies and babies, and I gratefully admit that, at one very important crisis in my life, I owed the preservation, if not of my sanity, at least of my sense of proportion, to a very young baby indeed. It was two months old, or thereabouts, and it lived by itself in the Bronx.

I was very down on my luck just then and I was feeling it rather badly. I got used to it very soon, thanks partly to the baby and partly to a policeman, as you shall hear; but at first I felt very lonely and that is quite the worst feature of being down on your luck. I am inclined to think, also, that for an Englishman, New York is one of the worst cities to choose for the purpose. I have tried several other capitals, Paris, Berlin, Rome and so on, but none of them affect me with quite the same sense of loneliness. Personally, I should not very much mind starving, or going to prison, or even, I daresay, being hanged, so long as the company was good. In Paris now, or Berlin, you do not expect company, good or bad. The people speak another language, look at life out of other eyes; to be lonely among them is no more than natural, just as it would be in a forest or a big field. To a New Yorker, I have no doubt London would seem just as lonely as does, or did, New York to me. As it happens, I am a Cockney, and when it comes to starving within the four-mile radius, I can always, at a pinch, find some one I know going through the same experience at the same time, and we can be bright and cheerful together and share our impressions, with our noses pressed against the same cook-shop window. So no doubt could a New Yorker, if he were a vagabond, in New York. And it came to me with a shock to find that in a city where my own language was spoken, with minor variations, and the people looked and thought and acted so very similarly to my own people, that I had no one, absolutely no one, with whom to share my lack of a good dinner.

I do not mean to say that I knew no one in New York. At the time I must have known at least half-a-dozen people, some of them, if not intimately, at least sufficiently to ask them for my passage back to England with a fair chance of getting it. I don't know, because I never tried, but I expect so. I did very nearly try, once. The man I thought of had an office, off Fifth Avenue, in the Thirties. I started off, three times, I think, or perhaps more, to call upon him. I was living up in a cheap hall-room on the North Side of Central Park at the time — and you have no idea what a long way it was to walk. The first time I did actually summon up courage to see him, and we had a pleasant chat together, and he asked me how I was getting on and I found myself telling him, quite involuntarily, of the lot I was thinking of buying on Fifth Avenue and the palace I was going to run up there when I could find time to think about choosing an architect. I tried, I suppose, a dozen times during that interview, to come to the point, and every time I got within half the dictionary of it my tongue shied and threw me and bolted off on its own account round a corner and out of sight. I gave it up at last and decided I would leave it until next day because there was just a chance that I might before then pick up a purse with a million dollars in it that some one had dropped in the street, and in that case, of course, I should have bothered my acquaintance unnecessarily.

I didn't find any purse and I started out to call on him next morning bright and early. I forced myself into the lift all right and into his office and he was out. I said I would call back in the afternoon, and I did, and I forced myself into the lift all right; but, when I got to the top, I couldn't force myself through the door, so I hung about the corridor for a bit and then went down again. And the next time I called I even funked entering the lift, and I knew by then that it was no good and if I wanted to raise money that way I should have to get somebody to do it for me.

I needn't go into the reasons why I was down on my luck just then, but I can time the moment when I really became a vagabond. It was the evening of my return from that office in the Thirties. It was about seven o'clock and I was making myself a cup of tea over the gas-stove when Mrs. Isaacs came in, to have a little business-chat. She was a very kind-hearted woman and I have no doubt I could have got round her again if I had tried hard enough. She didn't really give me a fair chance though, because almost at the beginning she told me that she had only trusted me so long because I was English — and that sort of thing.

I really believe she meant it, too — she had never let lodgings in England of course — so there was only one thing to be done. She let me stop there that night and in the morning we went into the value of what I had got left in the way of dressing-cases and clothes and things. She was much too generous; they were really worth uncommonly little, I fear, but it ended as satisfactorily to both parties as could be expected. We parted quite good friends, that is to say, and I had three dollars and no liabilities whatever. When it is a question of owing money that you can't pay I would very much rather have an American, and especially a Jewish-American as creditor, than an Englishman. I may of course have been lucky, but, as far as my experience goes, they do realise that it is possible to be hard-up without being necessarily a swindler, and that the hardest words cannot get money out of an empty

I was making myself a cup of tea over the gas-stove when Mrs. Isaacs came in to have a little business chat.

pocket. What is more, they put very much more faith in your word — especially, I honestly believe, if you are English. Mrs. Isaacs, for instance, was quite ready to let me depart and take my bag and baggage with me, if I would only promise to pay her when I could. I refused, for one thing because I didn't see the remotest chance of ever being able to pay her and, after what she had said, I didn't feel like bilking her; for another I didn't see what good a dressing-case and a portmanteau would be to me if I had nowhere to put them.

That morning I made the acquaintance of the Baby.

In the days before I became a vagabond I was very fond of going to the Bronx Zoo. I liked the beasts, and the gardens were charming, and I used to go with friends I was fond of and altogether I had very pleasant memories of the place. So while I was suffering under the first shock of realising exactly what those three dollars meant to me, I started out for the Bronx Zoo. I hadn't any reason that I know of; my mind had gone out of action for a time, and I suppose I went to the Elevated station and took my ticket and got down at the other end and walked into the Zoo quite automatically. At least I cannot remember going there, or how, or why. It was a bright, glittering day and I was mooning about, passively enjoying the sunshine and thinking of nothing at all, when suddenly, coming from somewhere very close at hand, I heard a sigh. It was quite the most melancholy sigh I ever heard, as though it was the outcome of bearing the whole weight of the world upon some one's shoulders. "O-o-gh-h-o-o!" it went, tailing away into a perfect infinity of weariness. "O-o-o-gh-o-o!"

Somebody was feeling pretty bad — that was obvious enough; who that somebody could be I had no idea. I was at the top of a little hillock, where four paths met; I could see round me clearly in every direction and there was not a soul in sight, man, woman or child, cat, dog or elephant. There was a bench-seat under a tree just behind me, and I found myself bending down to look under it in search of that mysterious misery. I was still bending, when I heard it again, more melancholy if possible than before. It came from behind me that time and I jumped round as though I thought some one was going to hit me.

In the angle formed by two of the paths was a low, wired enclosure, triangular in shape and about the size of a small room. The railing round it was not more than a couple of feet high and it was open to the sky, so it obviously did not contain any very savage or active beast. In the middle was a little round cemented pool and beside it, with its back to me, a low square wooden hutch. Evidently the sighing came from that. I had visions of finding a dying millionaire, kidnapped by toughs and left there to die, who, when I rescued him, would bless me with his last breath and press into my hand a purse containing several millions. I peered into the hutch just as another sigh came from it.

It was not a millionaire, at all; it was a baby sea-lion and it was very unhappy because it was lonely. I knew that at once, because as soon as it saw me it came waddling out of its hutch and romped. If you can imagine a black sleeping sack, made of American cloth and rather badly packed, romping, you will know what it looked like. It had an old, old face, hundreds of years old, and it had a shiny bald pate and it had whiskers and a healthy moustache, and it was really glad to see me. I thought at first it might be hungry, but it had a sufficiency of food at hand. It was only unhappy and lonely and wanting its mammy and feeling horribly small and insignificant in a great, hostile world that it couldn't understand, and dying for some one to talk to. I was feeling like that, too, and so we made friends at once and I have never had a truer friend or one who greeted me with more unfailing gladness or was more unfeignedly sorry when I left him. It wasn't cupboard love either, for I never gave him anything. He never thought of offering me anything — or I might have accepted it gladly. I called him Chris, after a former friend, because their eyes were very much alike.

We could never quite decide which of us had most to put up with. Chris had more food than he wanted and I had liberty; he was always longing to be back among the big waves and the ice-packs and I would have given a good deal to have some one to bring me my meals regularly. We had our loneliness in common.

Chris never knew how much he meant to me — in the way of giving me something to think of beside my own troubles. I worked out at least five distinct schemes for carrying him off and setting him at liberty in the Hudson. I would have done it, too, had I felt certain he would benefit by the change. But at that time I was realising rather fully that there are worse things in this world than a regular position, with a regular income attached to it, even if it meant being chained to a desk, or forced to adapt a round body to a square hutch — so I didn't. I feel sorry, sometimes, even now, that my heart failed me. Chris was delicate, the keeper told me, and they scarcely expected to raise him, so I suppose he is dead now and out of his troubles. He was very good to me, he was.

As long as my three dollars lasted I hung about the Bronx. It was bright, warm weather, and in the park and the woodlands round about it there was ample sleeping accommodation, and most of the daytime I spent talking to Chris — in a sort of dazed day-dream, not thinking at all, only feeling dimly that there wasn't anything particular to do or any particular reason to do it. By about the fourth day I began to re-orientate my position. Chris had taught me that I was not the only person in the world who had his difficulties and gradually it began to come over me that my position was really very much better than his, because he could not escape from his troubles, try how he would, and, if I would only try, I could. I waited until the Monday, because on the Sunday there were a great many people about, and we had very little chance of private talk together. On the Monday I bade him good-bye for the time, and he gave me all the encouragement he could think of, and as I walked away down the little hill he stood up on his tail against the railing and looked after me and rolled his head from side to side as though he were trying to wave his handkerchief to me.

It seems silly enough to look back to, but it felt uncommonly like saying good-bye to a friend. Some day, when I am very rich, I am going back to the Bronx Zoo — and if Chris is still alive I am going to buy him and take him back to somewhere in the Arctic Circle and there offer him the chance of his liberty. I don't believe he will take it, somehow.

I took the Elevated all the way down to the Battery, because it was so cheap, and I knew that there was the business end of New York, where I must look for a clerkship, or something of that sort, for I was not particular. The sight of the shipping-offices at the Bowling Green made me wonder whether I should not be wise to get myself shipped back to England as a pauper immigrant. But somehow the idea didn't smile upon me, especially when I thought of Chris. I couldn't find any work — you wouldn't be surprised, if you could know how shabby I was or how vague about my acquirements — and that night I slept upon a bench in Union Square.

CHAPTER II

On Sleeping Out

I HAVE starved in three capitals — London, Paris, and New York — but I was never so depressed in my life as to hear, when coming home to the Embankment recently, of the absurd new system they have started there. To wake a man out of a comfortable snooze and give him a ticket for a casual ward — as I understand is now being done — is to reduce starvation to an absurdity, to bring us all to the vulgar level of the small shopkeeper.

Hitherto, for general eligibility, London has been but a little way behind New York in the matter of sleeping out. To Paris I have never been partial; it is too full of adventure for a quiet man. There are at least as many unspeakables in London or New York, but they are for the most part opportunist; your Apache of Paris is a sportsman. There may be twenty thousand night-birds in either English-speaking city who would cut your throat for half-a-crown, but the half-crown is to them a necessary incidental. Without it you are safe from anything more than horseplay. But your Parisian murders from the sheer *joie de vivre.* You are to him no more than a head of game and the state of your pockets immaterial. I have known a man to be killed on the Boulevard de Clichy at three in the morning for not possessing a box of matches. And if you consider the kind of matches obtainable in Paris you can realise the significance of such an incident.

Compared with, say, Madison Square, I have always found the Embankment rather depressing. The company does not seem able to forget that it is under a cloud. It is down and out; it refuses to be proud of it. I am not sure that the coming of the all-night trams has not done something to improve this, by introducing a certain bustle; but at the same time it has diminished the chances of really refreshing sleep, chiefly because of the absurd arrangement of the roadway, by which groaning Juggernauts are made to rush by within a foot of your head. The police, too, have always been needlessly officious — perhaps as being under the immediate eye of New Scotland Yard. They manage these things better in New York.

There are three very good sleeping-out centres in New York — Madison Square, Union Square, and City Hall Park. They are strung, like beads on a rosary, at convenient distances along Broadway, so that if you get bored in the one, it is not too far to stroll along to another. There are other possibilities, of course — the Bronx, to which I have already referred, Central Park, or the Battery. But they are too far from the centre of things to be convenient. Central Park, again, is too lively — almost as bad as Hyde Park — and there is something suburban about it in suggestion. Personally, I would as soon sleep out on Turnham Green.

Each of my three chosen squares has its peculiar advantages. The benches of all alike are well designed, with backs at the proper angle. They are in some ways better than those on the Embankment, where, if you happen to get a corner seat, there is an unpleasantly sharp metal rim to the arm — in itself too sloping — which is awkward for your elbow. On the other hand, although you are in some danger of slipping off, the London design fits the small of the back, which New York ignores. As for Paris, you might as well try to sleep on a tombstone for any comfort you will get out of it.

City Hall Park is lively, Union Square is reposeful, Madison Square faintly aristocratic. City Hall Park has the newspaper offices, and is the best for a night when you are not sleepy and wish to be amused. My favourite pitch is the ring of benches round the fountain opposite the General Post Office. In hot weather little boys abound there, who use the basin as an open-air swimming bath at all hours, usually jumping in fully dressed — for what it implies — and having pleasant skirmishes with the not too officious police. The east side of Union

Square is quiet and well wooded — excellent when you are really tired; Madison Square, for some reason, attracts those who have seen better days. My last bench neighbour there was a British baronet, and dropped his aitches like a man. All three are open and free, without annoying railings or gates, well lighted by strong arc lights, with drinking fountains handy and lavatory accommodation fair for New York, where it is, generally speaking, abominable. All are on the main street-car lines, which run, however, discreetly after midnight, and thus are cheerful without being intrusive.

The company is delightful: optimists to a man and woman. I have talked to a hoary patriarch of, I suppose, seventy-five. He said he had not slept in a bed for ten years, and I believed him. Yet his whole conversation was on the best location for a motor works. He had invented, and had in his pocket, an entirely new system of electrical ignition — I am not an expert on these things — and when I left him he was figuring out the precise number of millions he would make when the factory was working at its full capacity. Every one has some scheme or other, and is quite ready to share it with you. The last time I slept in Union Square I was offered a partnership in one which I believe really had something in it. Some of the Elevated stations up-town are high above the streets over which they run — especially about the Cathedral Parkway — and they are approached from the roadway by long iron staircases, roofed in, so as almost to resemble tunnels. My neighbour's idea was to arrange a private company of three, two to hold up passengers — drunkards preferred — on their way down to the street, the third to keep watch. The working hours were from midnight to four in the morning and the probable returns magnificent. I did not accept the offer — as a matter of fact, before I had really time to consider it, I received another, which struck me as more promising, though, in the end, I did not accept that either. At least it is a fact that I never had such an offer on the Embankment; and now that they have turned it into a sort of annexe to the casual ward, I never shall.

CHAPTER III

Thieves' Kitchen

FEW things have made me realise more fully Man's superiority to the Beasts that Perish — I except Chris because he is my friend — than my own adaptability to circumstances. Granted the transportation of a lion to the Arctic Circle and I am ready to believe that in four or five generations he will evolve for himself the fur, claws and anatomy of a walrus, a Polar bear, or whatever other beast meets him half-way upon the path towards fitness. Mankind, if I am any example to go by, would reach the same point in four or five days. When I parted company with Mrs. Isaacs and my portmanteau I had all the prejudices of those born to the ringing of bells, as compared with those fated to the answering of them. It was certainly not the first time the wolf had curled himself upon my hearth-rug, but such earlier experiences differed in that they lacked the element of finality, that in every case the certain hope remained that either by coaxing or compulsion the wolf could sooner or later be expelled. But, as I sat on the benches of Union Square, it was unpleasantly brought home to me that the case was altered. Fortune, at whom I had so long made faces, was showing herself suddenly apt at the same game. No longer could I ring bells; I had not even the chance of answering them. Not only was I hungry, but gazing ahead I could see nothing but an eternity of empty stomachs. I was become, in earnest, the vagabond I had sometime played at being.

Within three days I adapted myself, unconsciously, to my new conditions. I gazed at a new world with new eyes and from a new angle. No longer was a policeman to me a henchman; he was become the Giant Corcoran, lord of dread powers, the more awful that their limits were to me unknown. No longer were clean faces and white linen the normal setting for humanity; they were mere abstract ideas, to be regarded from afar, lacking in actuality. I lounged upon my bench as though to the manner born, as though I had lounged there for long centuries, as though I had done nothing else this side the Blue Chamber of which Mr. Maeterlinck has told us. Then it was that the Tempter — as I am sure he would love to believe himself — came to me.

Not an hour after I was offered the chance of holding-up belated passengers on the Elevated came my introduction to the thieves' kitchen. I was sitting at the end of the bench nearest the central arc-light. I was sitting there the more easily to read, in a stray copy of the *Journal,* an article detailing the millions paid for a famous blue diamond, reputed to bring bad luck to its possessor, which yet had recently changed hands. There the Tempter found me. He was a small man, shabbily smart, and he told me that he was English. Then he sat down on the bench beside me — it was a little after three in the morning — and we chatted together, as one does on the benches of Union Square, without any formal introduction. He asked me several questions. He asked me if I was English and up against it, and I said I was both. Then he asked me if I would like to make some money, and I said there was nothing I should like better, except to have some given me. Then he asked if I was a University man and I said yes, but not of an English University, only German. He was a little disappointed at that, I could see, so I told him that I had a cousin who was at Balliol and who often let me speak to him. That cheered him up considerably and he said that if I liked to walk with him as far as Second Avenue it might be worth while. I was getting horribly tired of my own company by that time, so I went gladly.

We went into a saloon just off the avenue. We went in through the Family Entrance and into a sort of lobby lined with mirrors and through one of the mirrors, which were fitted so neatly together that you couldn't see any doors, into a little private room. There were two ladies and two gentlemen, and my friend the Tempter introduced me to one of the gentlemen, whose name was Mr. Birmingham. I am not using real names, of course, but they are near enough. Mr. Birmingham was what they would call in New York a near-gentleman, so near that you could scarcely tell the difference by artificial light. He was a good fellow, too, because when he asked me what I would take to drink, and I said I would much rather have something to eat, he was quite nice about it and sent out for a cold lunch of sliced sausages and dill pickles and crullers and things like that, and very glad I was to have them. Meanwhile he introduced me to his friend, whose name was O'Fallon and who was too shiny to be quite convincing, and to the two ladies, who only had given-names and for some reason, as soon as I spoke to them, began to laugh until they cracked their complexions. One of them was rather pretty and both were more fashionably dressed than seemed absolutely necessary. However, they were kind enough to say that I was some boob, or Rube, I am not quite sure which, as they were laughing so much, which I took to be complimentary. Mr. Birmingham, also, seemed struck with my appearance and intimated to the Tempter, whose name I gathered was Tripper, that he thought I should do. Then he asked me what my line was and I said that I was a teetotaller, which I wasn't, only I thought it seemed an appropriate thing to say and the two ladies laughed more than ever and one of them said that I was great.

Mr. O'Fallon for some reason did not seem to like me. He was rather a surly person who kept on muttering to himself under his breath, and at last beckoned Mr. Birmingham out of the room, leaving me alone with Mr. Tripper and the ladies. Mr. Tripper didn't seem very pleased with me either, I thought. He whispered to me something about not trying to put it over them too much, or something of that sort. The ladies kept on laughing all the time. They were very merry souls.

When Mr. Birmingham came back he got right down to business at once. He began by asking questions about my past career and future prospects, which I answered as untruthfully as was possible on such short notice. Then he asked if I had ever turned my thoughts towards bunco-steering or the green-goods game.

I do not know if it is necessary to explain that bunco-steering is what is known in England as the confidence trick, and is worked by forcing your acquaintance on a complete and guileless stranger and so gaining his confidence in one of many ways, that you induce him to hand over to you all his valuables, wherewith you then decamp. You may see it in operation almost any day in or about the big Strand hotels where Americans mostly congregate. For some reason Americans seem about the only people ever taken in by it. I am sure I don't know why.

The green-goods game consists in selling or pretending to sell forged United States banknotes —" green-backs," whence the name — to persons with more greed than honesty. Of course you profess to be able to supply them very much under the usual rates — ten cents on the dollar is, I think, customary. Equally, of course, you haven't any forged banknotes to sell at all, and you simply trick your customer out of his money. The ingenious part of the "game" is that, having himself embarked in a criminal business, he dare not afterwards prosecute you, and with any luck you can make further sums out of him in the way of blackmail. As you will understand, an appearance and manner of virtuous guilelessness is of great value in either of these "games," and I therefore felt that Mr. Birmingham's question was distinctly flattering.

He went on to point the moral by saying that being large and fat and fair, with a stupid face and an expression of blank idiocy, it struck him that Nature had cut me out for either — especially the first. I said that I had heard of them, but was not fully familiar with their details. He explained them to me carefully and added that if I took a hand in either I might very soon expect to attain a high position. At first I should have to start in a humbler capacity, merely to watch-out, when a game was in progress and make myself familiar with the faces of the slops who might be dangerous. Even so, he said, there was more dough to be made in a week than I could expect to earn in any other way in a year, supposing I ever managed to earn anything at all in New York. One thing only I must remember — and remember always. Obedience to orders — obedience and again obedience.

I am not at all sure that I should not have accepted the suggestion, had it not been for the presence of the ladies. As it was, it occurred to me that I should probably be expected to be on friendly terms with them and, somehow, I didn't feel like it. I doubted, too, whether I could ever really become intimate with Mr. O'Fallon. So I said I should like to think it over a little first. I said it with a certain diffidence, because I had visions, gained chiefly from the perusal of light literature, of being told to hold my hands up, knocked on the head, and dropped down a drain through a trap-door opening somewhere behind the fireplace. Nothing of the sort occurred. Mr. Tripper looked as if he was very sorry and Mr. O'Fallon looked as if he was very glad, and the two ladies laughed until the colour began to drop off their eyelashes, and Mr. Birmingham said that he could quite understand how I felt and that I could find him there any evening when I had made up my mind. Then we shook hands all round and I left them.

That was my only real experience of professional criminality in New York, and I feel myself that it was more than a little disappointing. If there had been only a pass-word or two, or a few oaths of inevitable vengeance if I played the part of traitor, I should have liked it better. But there was nothing of the sort, nor did I see so much as one revolver (technically known as "gun"), nor any masks, nor, indeed, any of the properly romantic accessories of crime. My friend Dempsey, who as a policeman himself should know something about it, told me later, when I discussed it with him, that Mr. Birmingham was probably brother-in-law to an Alderman and hand-in-glove with the superior officers of the police-force and that, did I attempt to betray them I should very likely be knocked on the head, not by the Criminal Band, but by a police-lieutenant on a charge of D. and D. It is true that Dempsey is something of a cynic and may have exaggerated. I only know that such was my introduction to the World of Crime and that if it is lacking in romantic features it is not my fault.

I had no regrets, for I got a square, if indigestible meal, out of it all, and just then I wanted one rather badly.

CHAPTER IV

The "Cop" and the "Copper"

I FIRST met Dempsey — as I will call him — when I was looking for the Bread Line. I had heard of it as offering the chance of something to eat, but I did not know its whereabouts. It was the second day after my interview with Mr. Birmingham and I happened to pass Dempsey, who was regulating the traffic at the corner of Broadway and Union Square and I asked him. Broadway belies its name at that point and the traffic was very heavy, but he found time to smile amiably, to ask me if I was up against it, and to lend me a pin, which I wanted urgently as I was unprovided with serviceable braces. Afterwards, in the intervals of dragging old ladies from under the wheels of street cars, he found more time to cheer me up, which I needed badly, to lend me fifty cents, which I needed more, and to tell me of a man who kept a delicatessen store on Sixth Avenue, and who needed an assistant. Officer Dempsey thought that if I said he had sent me, and that I could speak German, I might get the job. I did get it, and very interesting it proved, though that is beside the point for the present.

I do not for a moment say that the New York police force spends all its time in practising active benevolence towards needy foreign vagabonds, but this story happens to be true — and I have met nothing like it in London, Paris, Berlin, or Constantinople. No doubt Dempsey is an exceptional man; possibly he judged that I was not quite such a hobo as I looked; at least to me he typifies the whole splendid force of which he is a member. And I never read a little ha'penny press attack upon that force without wishing to mobilise a few corner-boys, toughs and gunmen, and to make a clean sweep of the particular office from which it originates. There is only one other policeman with whom it is not an insult to compare the New York "cop"—the London "copper,"—and the comparison is not altogether to the American's disadvantage.

I suppose it is because the Police Universal sees so much of the realities that it is ubiquitously benevolent, so far as my experience goes. The policeman of Paris is benevolent and inefficient; in Berlin, he is benevolent—yes, really—and officious; in Constantinople, benevolent and a fatalist; in London, benevolent and a snob; in New York, benevolent and a gentleman. Given two drunken seafarers fighting in the street who refuse to desist when challenged, the Paris policeman will pretend not to see them; the Berlin policeman will ring up a regiment of Uhlans; he of Constantinople will shrug his shoulders, cry aloud "Is this the will of Allah?" and proceed upon his beat with dignified aloofness. London and New York will alike arrest the combatants, or a dozen of them, single-handed, but London will consider whether they are admirals or deck-hands, and only use his truncheon in the latter case; New York will hammer either with equal joy. In other words, if you are unwillingly ragged beyond reason, London will arrest you for indecency; New York will lend you three pins and a piece of string. I can vouch for this, because at a time when I only possessed one pair of trousers, and they split — but I need not go into that. I do not blame London; the policeman merely honours the spirit of his nation; but so it is.

Granted, as I honestly believe, that the New York " cop " is, man to man, so nearly on an equality with his London brother, why is it that he gets all the kicks and his brother all the ha'pence? Simply because the Londoner is well officered, well supported, and sufficiently numerous; the New Yorker is none of these things. He suffers for the faults of his betters. I say this, not on my own authority, but on the strength of many facts, which I have seen and noted, and upon which Dempsey and his colleagues have commented with refreshing frankness, in my hearing.

There are at least as many — Dempsey says twice as many — criminals of the lowest type in New York as in London, Paris, and Berlin put together. I do not remember the exact figures, but there are fewer policemen in New York than in either. The "scum of South-eastern Europe," as President Wilson truthfully and rashly called them — and thereby risked a heavy loss of support during the recent presidential campaign — arrive in New York year after year in ever-increasing numbers, and stay there. The police force remains stationary, or nearly so. What is more, the policeman runs serious danger in arresting them, not from them but from his superiors. The magistracy is selected by and subservient to certain corrupt politicians of Albany and New York, whose personal retinue, for election and other purposes, is largely composed of gunmen and foreign criminals generally. Arrest a notorious criminal in the act, and as often as not, though you bring fifty witnesses of unimpeachable standing, he will be acquitted without a stain on his character. Let me again emphasise that these words are not my own, that the facts may not be as Dempsey believed. At least they are as he told them to me.

Such a state of things does not induce efficiency. Neither does the existence of the Mayor — as Mayors are understood in New York. It is perhaps worst when the Mayor is a politician; it is very little better when he is a reformer, which is to say a crank. In my time he was a senile person called Gaynor, with an itch for popularity and designs on the Presidency which, I am happy to think, came to nothing. In the case of any law which he thought unpopular he had a pleasant little habit of writing to the papers to the effect that he hoped the police would turn their blind eyes towards any breach of it. And the Mayor has more power over the police than has any Chief Commissioner. New York again, in common with the rest of America, is ridiculously over-lawed — with absurd little laws that are merely vexatious and do no good to anybody. Any crank with money and influence — which is the same thing — at Albany, the State Capital, can get any measure passed that he pleases — if he will but pay enough. Most of such laws are, of course, unworkable and unworked; they are nevertheless included, which is to say confused, with those really necessary to the public safety and convenience. The unhappy policeman has always to consider whether in enforcing the written law he may not be breaking one unwritten. I would not be a New York Policeman for a very great deal; I would very much rather borrow money from him.

Of the immediately superior officers, captains, lieutenants and the rest, we have been recently hearing so much that I need say little about them. I do not believe — neither does Dempsey, who knows what he is talking about — that the great majority of them are more corrupt than other men. Only — they all happen to be human beings, and some of them no doubt inherit their first ancestor's little weaknesses. We, after all, have had our own Piccadilly police scandals — and there are fifty Piccadillys in New York, forty or so concentrated in the one Tenderloin district. Do away with your politicians, your aldermen, your people with a pull, and especially your cranks, and there will be no need to talk of reforming the New York Police. The "cop" is drawn from much the same class as is the "copper." He is better educated; he has similar ideas of duty and he is as efficient to carry them out. Give him half a chance and he will make Heaven — even out of New York.

I know that this digression has little to do with my own vagabondage; but we hear so much, especially of course in England, of Dempsey's deficiencies and those of his officers that it seems only fair to remember that there is another side to the picture. Whether or no, I am sure of one thing: if Dempsey dies before I do, when I arrive in Purgatory I shall find him there, directing the traffic, and I shall trust myself to his care with absolute confidence that he will shepherd me safely past the Infernal trap-doors. What is more, he will be promoted Upstairs millions of years before most of those who now sit in judgment upon him.

CHAPTER V

The Free and Enlightened

SO far as I was ever an earnest politician, in New York or elsewhere, I became one through eating too much canned — or, as we should say, tinned — asparagus. It came about through my gaining the post of assistant to Mr.— I will call him Cholmondely, though his real name was very much more British and aristocratic — who kept a delicatessen store on Sixth Avenue, above Forty-second Street. My friend Dempsey, when he recommended me, told me that Mr. Cholmondely was a tightwad — and he was. He was an interesting combination, even for New York. His mother was Greek — a descendant of the Byzantine Emperors, as is every Greek in New York; his father was German — a descendant of the Emperor Frederick Barbarossa, as is every German in New York; and he was a Jew, and his name was Cholmondely, as I have said. He knew, because Dempsey told him, that I was "up against it." Dempsey lent me fifty cents, and it is always a pleasure to me to remember that however much I owed when I left New York I repaid him. Out of it I spent ten cents on getting my shoes polished, for dandy. It was really only five cents, but it was so long since I had had any money in my pocket that I slipped the guy a nickel — as we should say on the benches of Union Square — as a tip, and the accession of self-respect was worth it. Then I spent twenty-five cents on two collars — one must take some luggage on engaging new lodgings; and ten cents on a shave — the barber called it a hair-cut and wanted fifteen — so that I had exactly a nickel left when I took up my new position.

I hoped that Mr. Cholmondely would advance me something on my first week's salary, but he was of another opinion. If I had managed to live so long without, he thought I could last out another week and be spared the mortification of having to pay more than my salary back before I got it; which was logical enough. He liked the look of me, though, as he was kind enough to say, and he let me live on the surplus stock, on credit, for the first week. I spent my nickel on a loaf of bread, very good but painfully dear, and I made good on the surplus stock. It consisted of canned asparagus and sardines. If I live to be a hundred I never wish to see either of them again. They were bad enough separately; on the Thursday, having finished my loaf, I tried them together. On the Friday a dear little pantomime lady, who was engaged at a vaudeville house in the next block, said that for a fat man I was the hungriest-looking boob she had ever seen and asked me to have a sandwich with her. I had six and without shame; I told Mr. Cholmondely next morning that she was a principal, and that her credit was good, and it passed off all right. I have nothing against Mr. Cholmondely; he allowed me to sleep in the space behind the counter for the first week. I think it was harder, but it was very much more respectable than a bench on Union, or even on Madison, Square.

It was through Dempsey — my good angel — that I became a politician, though I honestly think I should have held back if it had not been for the asparagus.

I was alone in the store when Mr. Hawes came in. I had never before seen anybody who looked so prosperous. He had a big black moustache and a smile, a corporation, a diamond bosom-pin, and a cigar. He shook hands with me quite warmly and said he was glad to meet me. If you only knew what that meant to me! Then he said I was English. I hadn't had a chance to say a word, so I asked him how he knew. He said, because I dropped my aitches. Englishmen always did. Then to my surprise he ticked me off in a little note-book and said that my name was provisionally Alf Cohnstamm, a native of Paterson, New Jersey, and that I was to call at O'Keefe's café on Avenue A when I was sent for.

He was just bustling off when, I suppose, something in the voice with which I thanked him struck him as unusual. He looked at me rather queerly and asked me if I were a smart Aleck. I said that I did not know; that, from my name I imagined myself to be of Jewish descent. He still looked a little annoyed, so I smiled at him, and he relented and asked me if Mr. Cholmondely had not made me wise. I said that he had done his best — and that was really true, so far as the delicatessen trade goes. Mr. Hawes put his head on one side and shook hands again, quite warmly. They have a perfect mania for shaking hands in America. I have been told — though I do not know it for an actual fact — that as soon as you are born you celebrate the occasion by shaking hands with the accoucheur and that, if you are unlucky enough to be executed for murder — which you are not unless you are very unlucky indeed — you first shake hands with the electrician and the governor and the chaplain and the warders and the newspaper men, and tell them to be sure and drop in whenever they are passing. Anyway, Mr. Hawes shook hands

I was to call at O'Keefe's café when I was sent for.

with me twice and then, when he had already got as far as the door, came back and shook hands for the third time and said that I had got to quit kicking his dawg aroun', and that I was a bright-eyed mother's darling, and then the bosom-pin steered the cigar out on to the sidewalk.

When the chance came I asked Mr. Cholmondely about it, and he told me that mein roll was not zhick zat it might not be zhicker, and zat ze old Tiger was gut enough for him and for me, too.

A week later I was summoned to Mr. O'Keefe's café. Mr. O'Keefe was rather a bigger edition of Mr. Hawes, which was only natural, as he was a shade nearer the rose. His moustache and his smile and his corporation and his bosom-pin and his cigar were all a shade bigger and ranker, and he told me that I was a Democrat. I liked him at once, because he had bulgy purple eyes that looked as if it was only by the exercise of marvellous self-restraint that they did not jump out of his head, and reminded me of Chris, whom I was longing to see again, only the fare to the Bronx was five cents.

Mr. O'Keefe poured me out a chaser as he told me that I was a Democrat and he went on to say, with a chaser between each paragraph, that I was a fervent believer in

Smith for Mayor
And Jones for State Attorney
And some one else for something else.
And so were Mr. Breitstein
And Mr. Tuchverderber
And Mr. Letztergrosschen
And Mr. Mavrogordato
And Mr. Ferrati
And quite a number of other people
And that I was all of them

And that we were worth three dollars each for being what we were — a trifle under the usual rates because a large batch of emigrants had arrived a few days before and depressed the market.

Between surprise and the chasers and the

memory of the canned asparagus I believed everything that he told me.

In due course Mr. Breitstein and Mr. Ferrati and Mr. Mavrogordato and the rest of me all recorded our votes for Smith and Jones and the rest of the ticket. Incidentally, we made quite a lot of money out of our refusal to bolt, and I made up my mind to remain a Democrat for the rest of my life, or until the Republican rates became a shade less niggardly. I was glad of the money because, just about then, Mr. Cholmondely and I parted company and, until I got a job with the "movies" a month later I was rather badly unemployed.

CHAPTER VI

Business is Business

YOU have to pay ten cents in New York for a chicken sandwich, and it is usually made of turkey. You pay five cents for a ham sandwich, and you have no idea what it is made of. I was in the delicatessen trade in New York for three weeks — and I have my suspicions. For twenty-five cents you can have a club sandwich. That is made of toast and chicken-turkey and bacon, all hot and very good. It is well worth the extra expense, because the smell of the bacon disguises that of the chicken. American bacon is not good; it is nearly always sold in glass bottles, as we sell jam, which prevents its getting away. I prefer its flavour to that of delicatessen chicken, however, because I was in a hospital once and I hate being reminded of it.

Business is Business

There are as many delicatessen stores in New York as there are wine-shops in Paris or tailors in the City of London. To millions of good New Yorkers the most dazzling kind of orgy is to spend the evening in a cinema theatre, which costs five cents, and then go to a delicatessen store and have a ham sandwich. For the rest of the week you live upon dill pickles. Dill pickles are what we call gherkins, and they are far and away the most popular article of food in New York. You can get one for a cent; a really big and juicy one, which will do you for breakfast, with a bit over for lunch, costs two cents. The people of New York are simple and long suffering; the existence of the delicatessen store is the proof of it. In no other trade in the world can you make so large a profit with so little ruth. I should be in the trade now — and perhaps a millionaire — if it had not been for a chicken.

They sell chickens by the barrel in New York — wholesale, I mean — for much the same reason that they sell bacon in bottles. I was keeping store one day when Mr. Cholmondely came in in a state of great excitement. He had just heard of three barrels of chickens to be got at a bargain. They belonged to a big storekeeper, in a fashionable district up-town, who had quarrelled that morning with the Inspectors' Association — of which I will tell you more in a minute. As the result, they had to be sold at once, after being, I dare say, ten years in the family, and considered heirlooms. Mr. Cholmondely was anxious to get them before rival traders could hear of them. He didn't want to appear in the deal himself for political reasons, so I was to rush up at once and secure them. I forget the actual figures, but supposing the market price in the ordinary way would have been twenty dollars, I was to give three. It took me four hours bargaining and two interviews with the local Rabbi, but in the end I got them for three dollars and fifty cents, and Mr. Cholmondely very kindly offered to share half the loss with me. He even said he was pleased with me, and he showed it. I asked him if he would let me have a little money; I said I wanted to buy a collar. He wouldn't give me any money, because he said New York was full of temptations, but he very kindly offered me the loan of a used collar of his own, which he thought would pass for another day or two if I chalked it over in places; and when we found it wouldn't fit, he said I could take as much packing paper or string as was needed to eke it out and pay nothing.

There never was such a busy afternoon as we had when those chickens arrived. It meant no end of arithmetical calculations to start with, because to the cost of the chickens you had to add that of the chemicals, then to deduct the share of the value of those chickens that were so irretrievably gone that they could only be used for sausages or club sandwiches, next add the percentage of the inspector's fee, and finally average the whole thing over each chicken. We worked it out at a little over 450 per cent. profit.

We were in the middle of adapting the chickens to their new life; I was wearing the oxygen mask and coaxing them out of the barrels, and Mr. Cholmondely standing by with a club in case they turned nasty and attacked me, when the inspector came in. It worried me for the moment, and I wondered whether my employer would try to pass the barrels off as a soap-works or patent manure or something. He didn't, though. He handed the inspector a cigar, calculated to dominate even those chickens, and asked him to wait a bit. When he was ready he got a ten-dollar bill out of the cash register and handed it to him, and the inspector walked out. Mr. Cholmondely explained to me afterwards how these things are done in New York. There is an association of dishonest traders and another of dishonest inspectors — Inspectors of Nuisances I suppose we should call them over here — who regulate the amount of graft to be paid for each visit. (I don't mean to imply that there are no honest traders or honest inspectors either — but Mr. Cholmondely did not tell me about them. He was not interested in them.) In my time it worked out at ten dollars a visit, which was very moderate, considering that the trader can do anything he chooses in the way of selling rotten food, besides getting valuable hints as to the best kinds of preservatives and anti-stink chemicals and so on. If there is any dispute the associations settle it, and their word is final. If an inspector kicks he is bounced, and if a trader does he is prosecuted, and the newspapers marvel over the efficiency with which the people of New York are protected from the dangers of bad food. The system works admirably, and on the very few occasions it has broken down it has been almost entirely due to the mistakes of new assistants fresh from Europe, who do not understand business. For which reason Mr. Cholmondely explained that if ever a would-be assistant told him he was an honest man, he turned him down at once. He did not believe in taking risks, he said. I felt quite glad it had not occurred to me to lie to him.

We parted in the end over those same chickens. Mr. Cholmondely wanted me to take out part of my salary in club sandwiches, which he said I could eat at any time, and so not waste time over my meals. I had turned vegetarian by that time, and so I left.

CHAPTER VII

Among the "Movies"

I SUPPOSE there must be at least twice as many British baronets in New York as in London. I have foregathered with three in one night on the benches of Madison Square, where they mostly sleep. I have been told, though I cannot vouch for this, that on any fine afternoon hundreds of them may be seen in the Central Park Zoo, hungrily looking on while the animals are fed. In comparison, the sprinkling of honourables is but small, and in all my experience I met with but one peer. He was, when in employment, a collector for worthy causes, and he frankly admitted that his title was only assumed for philanthropic purposes. Next to the baronet the army captain holds pride of place. He has invariably served either in the Guards or the Lancers. I never met a British officer of any other grade or arm sleeping out, though I was for a few days on intimate terms with a field-marshal, who practised, I was told later, what would in London be known as the " kinchin lay "— stealing nickels from small children who had been sent on errands. He was, however, only a Cuban, and it was doubted in our set whether he really had the right to any rank higher than General.

When the New York press caricatures, intentionally or otherwise, the British aristocrat, it always represents him as being prejudiced against the letter " H." So widespread is this belief that when the Duke of Connaught, some time since, visited New York, those notabilities who saw any prospect of being presented to him spent hours beforehand practising aitchlessness, with the kindly desire to make him feel thoroughly at home. If you had met as many exiled British baronets as I have, you would understand the origin of this belief. When for a time I assumed a baronetcy I never could understand why the simplest-minded landlady recognised me at once for an impostor. Not until I had for three weeks acted as joint-assistant with another man of title to an Italian who kept a peanut stand at the corner of Twenty-third Street and Sixth Avenue did I discover that it was because I had not the proper accent, or perhaps I should say "eccent." When I say assistant, I should explain that the Italian was fond of his glass, and that Sir Alured — I mean my colleague — and I used alternately to mind the stand in his absence, and be rewarded with from two to three cents-worth of peanuts, according to time and business done. Peanuts are very satisfying, and for some time I lived literally on nothing else. Then I heard that it was forbidden to feed them to the squirrels in Central Park — because they were supposed to give them mange — so I decided to try a change of diet.

It was after I resigned my post in Mr. Cholmondely's delicatessen store that I went into the peanut trade. I should probably, with any luck, have had a stand of my own by this time had I not one day run up against a former customer, Miss Lamartine, as I will call her, of the vaudeville stage. She was the nice girl who had regaled me with sandwiches in Mr. Cholmondely's store, and when she heard that my whole worldly wealth consisted of three collars which I carried about in my pocket until I could afford to have them washed, she suggested that I should get work with the "movies." She was doing so already, and thought she could help me towards being taken on by the same people. I didn't quite know what "movies" were. I thought they had something to do either with the furniture trade or woollen underwear, but I jumped at the offer, especially when she told me it was worth three or even five dollars a day.

Theatre folk are proverbially generous, in New York as elsewhere. When we decided that my clothes were not calculated to inspire confidence, she took me to a former colleague who roomed on the East Side. As he had no more money than had she, he very kindly offered to lend me his only suit, which was extremely smart, in which to call upon the

Schutzenheimer Film Company — staying in bed until I came back. What he would have done if I had not come back, I tremble to think. I am glad to say, for the credit of England, that I resisted temptation. His clothes fitted me quite sufficiently well, considering my nationality — the average New Yorker has a prejudice against English tailoring, preferring something in which he can wrap himself five-fold against the cold blast of adversity — and I got the job.

The American stage is largely recruited by English actors who cannot make a living at home. When the English actor in New York fails in the legitimate — as is not infrequent — he recruits the "movies." There were many of him in the Schutzenheimer Company — along with a sprinkling of baronets and army captains.

I do not think I ever enjoyed a week more; there was only one drawback — a serious one it is true — the necessity of getting up at six in the morning. The Schutzenheimer studio was on the other side of the Hudson and work started at eight. They were doing a film of strong moral purpose that week, showing the evil results of gambling. In one scene the gambler wandered into a wood, I don't know why, and there fell asleep. A pitched battle took place over him between a legion of devils and his guardian angel. I was one of the devils, although the producer considered me rather stout for the part. I know I made an effective devil; my costume was black and skin-tight, and I wore horns and tail. The place where we did our scene was in the woods, about three miles from the studio. We went there ready made up, in the company's auto, and it broke down, so that we had to walk back. Miss Lamartine, who was the angel, and I got separated from the others, trying to find a short cut through the woods. After wandering for something like an hour we came across a row of unfinished houses. That part of New Jersey is in process of being developed as suburbs, so that unfinished roads and virgin forest are mixed up in the queerest way. We saw a workman doing something outside the last house, and I went up to ask him the way. As soon as he saw me he went down on his knees and explained that he had only taken such a little drop that it could hardly be considered backsliding at all, and that if I would only let him off this time he would never touch another drop as long as he lived. When Miss Lamartine came up, all in white with golden wings behind her, he began to weep with joy and gratitude that his prayer had been answered.

It was my own fault that I did not stay with the Schutzenheimers. I found, though, that the only way I could get up early enough to catch the seven o'clock ferry boat was by sitting up all night beforehand. One of the men in the company gave me an introduction to a man who had a booth at Coney Island, opposite Luna Park, and wanted a Hindu magician in a hurry. The pay was less than I was making, but I didn't have to start work till three in the afternoon, so I applied for the place and got it.

CHAPTER VIII

Coney Island

IF you take Earl's Court, Shepherd's Bush, Blackpool, Douglas, I. O. M., and the Hammersmith Broadway on a Saturday night; arrange them along both sides of a street a little broader than Kingsway and perhaps three times as long, and a multitude of little alleys, for footpassengers only, leading from it to the sea; set the whole down somewhere beyond Shoeburyness in the Essex Marshes and fill up the space between it and London with unfinished suburbs of the cheaper kind — say Cricklewood, only built of wood instead of red brick — you will have a very faint approximation of Coney Island, where I was for a time a Hindu magician.

In the elaborate works of art which covered the front of the marquee wherein I performed my miracles, I was pictured as a high-caste Brahmin. I was also represented as having a long white beard and as sitting on a carpet surrounded by Oriental houris. In actual fact I had no beard and there was a distressing lack of houris. Instead, there was a bearded lady — quite genuine and rather pathetic, seeing that she powdered the upper part of her face with an eager earnestness that overran its purpose — a lady with four legs, the thinnest man on earth, the most despondent giant — or so I suppose — on earth; two horribly deformed negresses, described as bear-women, and a snake-charmer, reputed Oriental, but not answering the description of a houri.

We were displayed upon platforms ranged round the interior of the marquee, each about the size of a large dining-table; and at ten-minute intervals a lecturer came round and described us to those members of the public who paid a dime admission. From him they learnt that, as well as a magician and a Brahmin of the highest caste, I was a fakir and a guru. To be quite truthful I myself suggested to him that

I should be a guru, and the idea appealed to him. We neither of us knew what the word meant — not, I hope, anything improper — but it had an Oriental atmosphere about it. I was the intimate of a long line of Viceroys; I had cured the late King Edward, Kaiser Wilhelm, and the President of the Swiss Republic of tic-douloureux in its most advanced stage; I had been visiting the western slopes of the Rocky Mountains in search of curative herbs, and, on my homeward journey to Mofusselbad, I had been prevailed upon, at enormous expense, to break my journey at Coney Island. My salary was $12 a week and two meals a day, with the privilege of sleeping in the marquee at moments of financial stress, but this the lecturer did not mention.

My more immediate purpose was to sell little bottles of toothache tincture at the reduced price of a dime each — never retailed to crowned heads at less than a hundred dollars, and then only to potentates in reduced circumstances. Towards this end I had a turban, an olive complexion, a tom-tom, upon which I beat

From him they learned that, as well as a magician and a Brahmin of the highest caste, I was a fakir and a guru.

with my fists at slack moments, and an Oriental prayer, which I intoned upon my knees, beating the floor with my forehead and raising my hands heavenwards alternately. It was a very good prayer, and had an excellent effect. It was a very good toothache tincture, too; I made it myself in full view of the audience, from a large white root that looked like cheese and smelt like a pig's idea of Paradise. I boiled it in a lotah — I called it a loofah several times, by mistake — over a charcoal brazier. I used to address the audience in flowery English — a really moving address, that had been written for Mr. Czartorisky, my proprietor, by a member of the staff of the *New York American.* As a rule, the audience were quite satisfied with it, but one evening a young gentleman of the kind ticketed in New York as a " smart Aleck," spoke to me in my native tongue. He had a young lady with him, to whom he loudly described me as a fraud, which annoyed me, considering how hard I was working for my living. He said that he had lived for quite a time in Calcutta. The young lady suggested that he should expose me, and he came forward for that purpose, while the crowd stood round expectant. I felt the lecturer behind me tremble so that the platform shook, but I was not alarmed. I caught an appealing expression in the young man's eye more expressive than many marconigrams. Accordingly, when he spoke to me in unknown tongues, I replied to him in a variation of Hindu which surprised even myself. We had quite a pleasant little chat, to the admiration of the beholders, after which I saluted him in English, as " Lord Sahib," and told him that he reminded me of Lord Curzon, who had bought two dozen bottles of my specific, and that I hoped he would do no less. He was quite a nice boy; he bought a dozen bottles there and then and gave me a five-dollar bill for them — at least a third of his weekly salary, I suppose. If you had seen the look in the young lady's eyes, though, you would have realised that it was well worth it to him. I salaamed to him as he turned away, purple with joy, and called him " Lord Sahib of all the Elephants "— and the young lady kissed him even before they had left the tent. The rest of the audience cheered, and in about five minutes I had sold out my whole stock. They are simple souls, the Great American People, even simpler, I think, than the English. I will not say that they are without forethought, though. I had two written proposals of marriage the first week, and both insisted that I should put away any other wives I might already have in India. One lady added that I must never expect her to ride on a camel.

We were really a very happy little family, and some of the supper-parties we used to have in the marquee after closing hours — which is to say about one in the morning — were perfect Agapes. Czartorisky, who was much too generous ever to be a successful man, I fear, provided the fare, which was always the same — beer, Frankfurters, and boiled corn. These are the staple dishes at Coney Island; there must be a thousand establishments, I suppose, devoted to the sale of " Domestic " Frankfurters in Coney Island, not a very large number either, if you remember that in a successful sea-son they have crowds running into the seven figures in the course of a day, and that every one of them eats at least one Frankfurter.

I was — and knew that I was — a fool to throw up such a job, but the truth of the matter was that I could not stand the Bear-women. I don't know that I am more squeamish than another, but there was something so horrible about their deformities that I used to squirm every time I saw them. I thought I should get used to it, but I didn't somehow, and in some extraordinary way they got to like me — they were sisters — and used to come and talk to me at odd moments.

I stood it for three weeks — and that really was a continued act of heroism, although I say it myself — and then the lady with four legs began to discuss the works of Mr. Arnold Bennett with me — (this is quite true, although you will not believe a word of it) — and the combination was too much. I told Mr. Czartorisky about it and he understood — he was a white man all through and a gentleman — and he introduced me, over a "clam-bake" dinner on the sea-front, to a business acquaintance, who ran one of the saddest little circuses you ever saw in your life. He said — and I really believe that for the moment he believed it himself — that I had a life-long acquaintance with the East Indies and was a natural-born mahout. I mention this because it shows that Mr. Czartorisky was a poet and an artist. His friend, whose name was Wolff, had an elephant — such a sad, pathetic little elephant, as you shall hear — named, of all names in the world, Gladys, and he was anxious about her health. He thought she was fretting — which was not at all unlikely considering that her mission in life was to balance herself ungracefully upon a large wooden ball and fit herself, disgracefully, into a chair and pretend that she was drinking champagne. So he engaged me as her attendant, to double the part, so to put it, with that of assistant-groom to Danny, who was a mule and was advertised as the strongest kicking mule in the world, with a standing offer of fifty cents to any member of the audience who should succeed in sitting him twice round the ring.

CHAPTER IX

"Gladys"

IF I had been Mr. Wolff I do not think I should have engaged me to act as attendant to Gladys. Not, at any rate, to appear publicly in that capacity. I freely admit that I am large, for my species — both in length and depth and width. Gladys, on the other hand, was distinctly small. She was an elephant all right, because she had a trunk. She was an African elephant, too, as her ears witnessed — although I have been told that African elephants are untamable. On the other hand, African elephants have large ears and, at the risk of being accused of exaggeration, I can only say that her ears were so large that, had she been only a foot or two smaller, and accustomed to hang upside down from one foot, she could easily have passed as a bat. We got so fond of each other that I sometimes used to feel that I was unfaithful to poor Chris.

I never became really intimate with Danny. For one thing he had a distorted sense of humour and a long reach. He could kick all round him with each leg separately or all together, and when he hit you he hurt. He was a consummate hypocrite. One particular trick of which he was very fond was to pretend that he was an amiable horse muzzling his nose into your pocket in search of a carrot. He didn't want any carrot in reality. He didn't like them. He very much preferred a plug of chewing tobacco. What he wanted was a bit of you, and when he had got that he would go off into a perfect volley of malicious laughter in case you should miss the point of the joke. I will say for him, though, that with all his little faults of character he was a conscientious workman. Mr. Wolff might safely have offered five hundred dollars to whoever could ride him twice round the ring against his will; even a monkey couldn't sit him for two minutes and we had one monkey, called Ipecachuana, who was the best rider I ever saw. It was really a pleasure to see Danny get to work. He would start with two or three harmless buckings, to give the enemy confidence. Then he would drop his head until his nose touched the sawdust, stand on three legs and use the fourth — it was immaterial which, though he got the prettiest action out of his off hind foot — as a rake or comb or whatever you like to call it. He would begin along one side, to stretch his muscles a bit and worry his rider, and he would gradually work upwards until there was not an inch of his own backbone, from withers to tail, that had not been explored by that extremely quick-action hoof. I haven't the least doubt he could have combed himself down the other side as well, if he had felt like it, but he never needed to. His enemy was always outside the ring by that time.

He had the artistic temperament, had Danny, with all that it implies for good and evil. One way in which he showed it was his method of entering the ring. He was never the same in any two performances, always altering and improving and experimenting towards the perfection of his art. Sometimes he would adopt the despondent suggestion of a broken-down cab-horse, tottering sluggishly into the ring and standing there awaiting trouble — the other man's trouble — the very picture of despondency. He even used to keep his eyes shut — or that one which was towards the audience — to veil the red light of savage anticipation within them. Another time he would rush into action like an embattled volcano, eyes blazing, ears laid so far back that you could not see them, mouth wide open and every hair on his hide standing up in separate defiance. Then he would rollick round and round the ring, daring any one to come within five foot of his four.

There was only one weak spot in Danny, regarded in the light of a money-maker, and that was his independent spirit. Even in my limited period of acquaintanceship with him he three or four times played Mr. Wolff the nasty trick of pretending that he was a sheep. He would amble into the ring with an air of the sweetest reasonableness and there he would stand until a boy got on his back. Then, while we were all watching-out to catch the boy when the explosion should take place, he would surprise us by ambling gently round the ring, doing everything that his rider told him and finally standing still for him to dismount, with the expression on his hypocritical face of a well-trained butler conscious of having done his best. It used to annoy Mr. Wolff quite considerably; but it was really very good for trade, because it encouraged other boys to try their luck and he never did the ambling palfrey act twice in one week.

It was as well that we had Danny to liven things up a bit; apart from him I suppose we were the most despondent sort of circus that ever tried to exist. And Gladys was the most despondent creature in it. Nature never intended her for a circus-performer; she ought to have been a nun, attached to some Order where she was allowed melancholy love affairs with consumptive young boy-elephants and given stated hours for weeping over their early graves. Failing that she ought to have been a char-woman — or as we should say in America, a scrub-lady — with a husband who beat her, and eight children. She had very little hair, but she carried the permanent suggestion that she never put it up properly, only made it into an unkempt wisp when she got up in the morning, and left the rest to Providence. I always think of her now as wearing a rusty black bonnet with strings and as shedding tears.

I never knew for certain, but I think she must have had an unhappy love-affair with the man who preceded me as her mahout. I think that he borrowed all her money, under promise of marriage and forgot to pay it back before he left. If it were so, I am not sure that the blame was altogether his. I think he must have been sorely tempted. Before I had known her three days she signified to me in the usual manner that her heart was mine alone and only mine. She used to put her trunk round my waist and whisper her troubles into my ear and when she felt sure that I was what the Italians would call *simpatica,* she tried to climb onto my knee and lean her head on my shoulder.

I have never been able to make sure whether she suffered from stage-fright or was merely incompetent. Sometimes — about once in five attempts — she would go through her act quite perfectly; sit upon her chair, if not gracefully, at least solidly; raise herself up on end, placing one foot on the table; ring her bell with a certain dignity and, when I brought her the Indian club wrapped in silver-foil that passed for her champagne bottle, drink from it at least as convincingly as you could expect from any untutored African ingénue. But — the odd four appearances could only be described as tragic fiascos. Either she would go on her knees and look at me out of the corners of her eyes — they were small and red and rather piggy — so appealingly that members of the S. P. C. A. who happened to be present would be stirred to instant action, or else she would seize her hand-bell, give it one tragic, despairing clang, attempt to drink out of it, as though she thought it was her champagne bottle and then promptly lie down — a performance that was not expected of her until the end of her act — and refuse to get up, whatever the means of compulsion, until the five bears, introduced by the Signora Esmeralda, who was really Mrs. Wolff under another name, were half-way through their melancholy pretence at gymnastics. She would confide to me afterwards, as I led her to the canvas stable which she shared with Danny and the three pie-balds, and Senor Vivaldas' monkeys, and Joey the vulgar donkey — that she was a *femme incompromise* — her French was not very good — and that until Women got the vote — and things like that. I believe so, at least, because grief usually made her incoherent and she was feeling for bits of sugar — which she did not deserve — in all my pockets while she spoke.

If Mr. Wolff had been the ordinary kind of circus-proprietor I should certainly have got the sack within a week of my enlistment under his banner. Fortunately for me — for I was very happy with him — he was not. His ambition was to be a minister. I know it sounds as if I were making this up, but I am not — and anyone who performed at Coney Island in the spring of 1912 can tell you so. He was quite a young man and he had studied theology somewhere in Mamaroneck, New York, and if he had not married, I think — from what I know of him — that he would be studying there now.

Before her marriage Mrs. Wolff was a school-teacher. She was the niece of the original proprietor of the circus, but she was not on visiting-terms with him, because her mother held that circuses were immoral. Her husband agreed with her mother, and I have no doubt that she agreed with her husband and listened to his prosy arguments on the Whole Duty of Man with all the earnest-eyed adoration into which a really nice girl can persuade herself when she is in love. They had been married about six months — starving genteely, I suppose, most of the time — when the uncle died and left her the circus. Mr. Wolff would have flinched from the responsibility and attributed his cowardice to high moral tone. Mrs. Wolff did not. She pointed out to him — of course I was not present, but so I believe — that if the affair were sold up at once it would bring in enough to support them — and a probable third person — for about a fortnight. If it were run as a going concern and with ability, enough might in the end be made out of it for him to be able to afford to enter the ministry.

Mrs. Wolff was raised somewhere in the back-blocks of Vermont, which is to say that she was a young woman of New England; which is to say that she had ideas on the proprieties and the respectabilities and the decencies which you will find nowhere else in the world, except perhaps in parts of Surbiton and Croydon and the lower end of the Balham High Road. When I joined the aggregation they had been running it for just over a year, and she used to put five sad-eyed bears through their paces three times a day. They were dressed for soldiers and she wore a very smart vivandière's costume and very pretty she looked in it. She was not a good bear-leader. She has told me herself that she was horribly afraid of the bears at first, ragged and depressed and lacking in enterprise as they were. The costume outraged all her sensibilities, also — but she was up against it, and she meant to make good and she did. That was the sort of woman she was. The original Signora Esmeralda — I imagine that she was something of a hussy, though I never saw her — was receiving thirty dollars a week and extras. When the concern changed hands she thought she saw her opportunity for blackmail and demanded seventy-five. Mr. Wolff would have given it her, to save trouble. Mrs. Wolff got rid of the Signora at short notice, carried out some legal arrangement that vested in her the ownership of the dismal troupe and herself assumed the vacant leadership.

I am not a New England school-marm, and I have no objection to fancy dress or the smell of sawdust, and I am not afraid of bears, at least of mangy, melancholy bears without a decent claw-stroke among them — so I cannot myself realise all that it must have meant to Mrs. Wolff. But I can imagine it. It was not all she did either, by a long way. She had a very small pink son, called Tobias, and she used to mother him and see to all the business side of the affair, and run the staff and book the tours and make contracts for hay, and do a hundred other things as well. Her husband had a little canvas room just behind the stables and he spent nearly all his time in it. I think he used to pray there, and I know he was writing a book on the most profitable Way of Conversion, because as soon as he found that I had lived for a time in Wales — which is where all the best brands of religion come from nowadays — he insisted on reading some of it to me. He was disappointed in me at first, because Czartorisky had — with the kindest intentions — given him the impression that during my long years of residence at Mofusselbad I had become slightly tainted with Buddhism, and he scented a shining reconversion.

Mr. Wolff did not convert me to anything; Mrs. Wolff made me a feminist and a suffragist and at Mrs. Pankhurst's service whenever she cares to call upon me. Even Gladys, who is, I suppose, the most feminine creature with whom I ever foregathered, was never again able to rouse in me the Pride of Manhood. That was a good proof of the sincerity of my conversion because, disregarding the proprieties, we used to take exercise together on the sands of Coney Island in the very early morning. We used to walk arm-in-trunk, picking our way among the thousands of New Yorkers who find there cheap sleeping-places during the warmer months. Gladys, holding the tip of her trunk so that I could not escape a word of it, used to open her heart to me — and even so I am still a suffragist.

I remained associated with Wolff's Mammoth Hippodrome and Concise Compendium of the World's Most Marvellous Miracles until it again changed hands. It happened not very far from a place called Montauk, which is at the furthest extremity of Long Island and quite a long way from New York, so I suppose that I ought not to include it in these reminis-

, We used to take exercise together on the sands of Coney Island in the very early morning.

cences. As however the reader who has accompanied me so far has already paid, I am not unduly worried.

We were performing in a certain village, the name of which I will not mention, when Mr. Wolff got a call. I don't know how he got it, because I was down at the railroad depot at the time, seeing after a shipment of hay that had gone astray; and before I got back Mrs. Wolff had arranged everything, sold the whole concern over the telephone as it stood, settled all the bills, given us all formal notice, interviewed a doctor about some childish trouble — I think it was croup or convulsions or something of that sort with which Master Tobias was experimenting — and was looking up the times of the boats from Montauk Point to somewhere in Connecticut where the call came from.

She had grown quite fond of her bears by that time and felt she couldn't part with them, so she excepted them from the sale and took them with her. I often used to wonder what the congregation thought of them.

CHAPTER X

"Who's Got the Button?"

I MIGHT have remained with the Compendium under the new proprietary, but somehow I did not feel anxious to do so. I was sorry to part with Gladys; I am bound to say that she showed few signs of grief at losing me, displaying instead, when I introduced her new mahout, a deeper interest in the contents of the new Amurath's pockets than in the farewells of the old. I do not blame her, the less so that when I again met with her, by chance, in Paterson, New Jersey, some months later, she indubitably recognised me — her trunk-tip darting as undeviatingly towards the pocket in which I used to keep the sugar as does an arrow towards its goal. She was of a different temperament to Chris. On my return to New York I paid him an early visit and he positively howled with delight on seeing me again. I very nearly did myself, so honours were easy.

I had thirty dollars in my pocket when I parted brass-rags with the Wolffs, and quite an album of photo-postcards. It was characteristic that those representing Mr. Wolff all showed him in clerical guise; poring over a massive tome; raising his eyes heavenwards in ecstatic thought or, in one of which he was very proud, in prayer before a mahogany tallboy — the shoe-heels rather larger than life owing to perspective difficulties. This last he autographed as " Rev. Meander S. Wolff." His wife preferred to be remembered in my mind in two alternative aspects — as Vivandière, putting her bears through their exercises; and as Mother, yearning over her first-born with that intensity, photographically sacred to maternity, which suggests the fear that the first-born is going to be sick and spoil the picture. They were very good people, the Wolffs, and if I ever enter Heaven I shall expect to meet him there. I am not so sure about his wife, because I know she will insist on taking her bears with her and if any officious archangels are about, difficulties may result. Perhaps, though, she will succeed in passing them off as those that ate up the small boys who told the bald-headed prophet to go up.

I decided to walk back to New York, because when you have money in your pocket you feel that it is unfair to others less happily situated to spoil the market. I had not gone twenty miles on my homeward way before I fell in love and stayed there — *in situ* I mean. I did not fall in love with one woman, but with two, I suppose I ought to be ashamed to say. It happened at Hopkins's, which is within a thousand miles of Good Ground, which is in Long Island and would be ideal were it not infested with golfers. Hopkins's stands in a wood a couple of miles away from the golfers and I have never seen a prettier place, nor one that more completely satisfied the desire occasionally felt, even by those of us who are vagabonds, for a place where one could really settle down and be at rest. Its first attraction to me was a little runnel of water, springing up out of nowhere and dimpling along over a natural carpet of grass. I was thirsty and I bent down to drink, and while I was drinking a large buck nigger fell upon me — literally I mean — out of a cherry-tree. He did not hurt me at all, but we rolled over and over together in the runlet, and in due course I held his head under it until I thought he was drowned — and then Sarah and Billy appeared.

I didn't know who they were and they certainly didn't know who I was, and as they came up to where I sat, vilifying my Maker, on the edge of the runlet, they held out fat podgy fists, rigidly clasped, towards me — and I am bound to confess, also towards the nigger, who was squattering on the bank like a wounded duck — and they said "Button — Button — Who's got the button?" They said it in the queer little high-piped voice of childhood that is sometimes an ecstasy and sometimes an intolerable pain — according to what you have been doing for the last six months or so.

I was not initiated about the button, but I felt it would be right to extend my hands as they did — and Sarah dropped something into my palm and pouted. "He's got the button," she said — and I certainly had, and it was evidently part of the game that if you had the button you lost the game. It was a little white button. I have still got it.

Sarah was two and a half and Billy was a year older, and they had ordered Jake, who was the nigger, into the cherry-tree to pick them cherries. And because they were Billy and Sarah he had gone, although it was weeks after the last cherry had been picked — and if you had been there you would have done the same. Billy, let me say, was a young lady. She it was who continued the conversation. "I said something very funny just now," she confided to me, with a shade of abruptness in her manner.

I suppose I looked interested, for she did not wait for a reply. "I said Dod," she exclaimed. "And it means, 'Tumble *right* down.'"

"Who's Got the Button?"

As I have already said I do not know that I am partial to babies. As a rule I prefer elephants, because you are not afraid to lecture them if they annoy you. But I certainly did like Billy and Sarah. They were not babies, for one thing, they were whole millions of years old — you had only to see them walk to be sure of it. They always walked together, hand-in-hand rather stiffly and with a certain care. They were not particularly pretty — as I have been told by neighbouring mothers — but they had little twiny fingers that used to twist round yours very trustfully, and big round eyes that when they caught yours used to make something click inside you, and I know in my heart, although he never admitted it, that Jake tumbled from the cherry-tree on top of me — although he saw that I was white and large and that trouble would ensue — because he thought that it would make them laugh. It did not — I never knew them to laugh except at inward thoughts of their own which they never shared with mere mortals — but it was worth the risk. I did much more absurd things myself before I had done with them — and I am a very clever man and they no more than farmer's brats. I forget if I mentioned that I have got that button still.

I wasn't a hobo just then, and I was not looking out for the chance of doing "chores" but I really had no say in the matter. They walked very stiffly, one on each side of me — as I suppose the angels do when you are trying to dodge Saint Peter — and after exactly ten steps, as if they were doing it to signal, each took one of my hands — they had soft little fingers, as I have said, of the sort that make you wish you had married decently twenty years ago and had a safe job in a bank. We made a little procession — Jake, who was already murderously jealous, following behind — to an old frame house that was covered over from roof-tree to ground with wistaria boughs. It stood in a little grove of its own, all wedged in among bright flowers, most of them purple and blue, with a very strong sunlight shining down on them, and brown fields and woods just thinking about getting golden.

We went in by a back door — it was none of my doing — and just before we entered I half turned my head for some reason that I don't remember, and I saw a blue vision of sea slither up among the trees. As we get older we remember things more by little impressionist pictures than as actual happenings. The sea, as I have said, was blue — real blue — and there was a false blue — some kind of a flower I suppose — just beside it and a touch of pearl colour above it edged with golden pink, and the grey door opening slowly, and rich umber within and a face — it seemed ash-colour — watching out of it. The children were there also in the picture, although I wasn't looking at them and could not see them. They were of some warm colour that filled up the edges. I often see it now — although I am living in Chelsea and have no other outlook than the chimney-pots over the way. Even Jake — who was five feet behind me and clamantly invisible — enters that picture as a sort of brown smudge.

The face was that of the mother, who was

named Mrs. Hopkins and whose husband was a farmer. Our introduction was "He's got the button" and I am inclined to think that the same thing had happened before, because Mrs. Hopkins took everything for granted, and told me that I could sleep in the barn, before I had broached any subject at all. We had prayers that night — the family and Jake and a girl and two hired men — and I slept like a lamb and woke at four in the morning, which as it turned out was exactly the time I was supposed to wake and gave Mr. Hopkins a very good opinion of me. I expect that Sarah — who was the more mystical of the two — rang up one of her particular friends among the angels and told him about me and that I was not naturally an early riser.

I am not going to tell you any more about Billy and Sarah because I should hate to be thought a sentimentalist. Like Jacob I served three weeks for Sarah and another three weeks for Billy, hewing wood and drawing water, and one morning I realised that I was in danger of catching the prevalent American disease —

sentimentality — and I chose a moment when I knew that Billy and Sarah were busy with the tortoise, and I drew my money and left. I don't know whether the tortoise was wild or domesticated, whether he just grew or whether he had escaped from somewhere, but we found him, we three, on the edge of the runlet one morning when I was supposed to be chopping wood in the barn, and I made a little hole in his shell and put a bit of string through it and we tethered him there and called him Alphonso — at least I did; Billy and Sarah called him Funs — and we made a little dam across the runlet with clay and branches in case he should want a swim, which I don't think he ever did, and we made up a story about his being a Spanish Prince, who was looking for the Princess Bright-Eyes, and had been turned into a tortoise by a Wicked Witch, and we spent a great deal of our time there safeguarding him against further enchantment.

I left by the path that went through the wood and past the spring-head and as I walked along I saw two little figures in blue overalls and two little flaxen heads very close together bending down over the runlet — and since I got back to England quite a number of asses have condoled with me over the hard times I had in America.

CHAPTER XI

A Pair of Boots

WHEN I have made my fortune and buy America I am going to reserve Long Island for my private residence and divide the rest among my friends. I do not say it is the most beautiful or desirable place in the Continent, because there are some parts that I don't know; but it happens to please me best and as I shall be paying the piper I see no reason why I should not call the tune. My chief residence will be somewhere very near Amicus and for the same reason; I don't say it is the most beautiful part of the Island — as a matter of fact, it is not — but I have very pleasant memories of it indeed. It is not called Amicus, but something rather like it.

I arrived in Amicus on foot, but as I had

nearly forty dollars in my pocket I put up at an hotel. It was not one of the big summer palaces down on the Ocean-shore, but a very pleasant, old-fashioned place near the railroad depot, with a dear old landlady who mothered you, and who took no end of trouble to find the store where they sold exactly the brand of dentifrice you liked best, and who had a husband who used to come into your bedroom in the morning before you were up and sit on the edge of the bed and discuss the latest murder with you. His way of discussion was rather unusual. He would begin, as if he were a newspaper headline. "Love drama in Hoboken. Octogenarian millionaire asphyxiated. William J. Jones — wife's sister's son suspected." When he had said that he would put something into his mouth and ruminate. I never found out what it was — chewing gum, I think — but at least he never spat, although sometimes he would wander away towards the window and take whatever it was out of his mouth and look at it very carefully as though it were a clue, and then put it back again and sit down on the edge of the bed and resume the discussion. I don't mean that he said anything. As a matter of fact he never spoke; only stared very hard at a text hung over in one corner of the room, with his head up so that you could see the veins and muscles of his throat working under his chin-beard in time to the great thoughts that were pouring off him. After about ten minutes he would get up and go away; and I know that he thought well of me, because he afterwards got me a job and he told the other man that I was the brightest talker he had ever known — although, beyond "Good-morning" and "Good-night," I really do not think I ever said twenty words to him.

It was not until some weeks later that I understood why we always discussed murders. It came about because I bought a pair of shoes or, as we should call them, boots. I was wearing, and had been for weeks past, a pair of patent-leather Oxfords or, as we should say, shoes. They were intolerably outworn, but they were very comfortable and somehow I had got it so firmly fixed into my head that I could not afford to buy any others, that I just went on wearing them, even when I had money in my pocket. They cracked very badly — I do not blame their maker because they were never intended for heavy wear. They had thirty-eight large cracks — besides the gaping abyss behind the left toe-cap, which stood in a class by itself — and a whole network of little ones — at the time I parted with them. I dropped them into the clear water of the lagoon and three weeks later, when I passed over the same spot in a motor-launch, some kind of a deep-sea beast — a hermit crab, I suppose — had made his home in one of them and was complaining bitterly to his friends about the draughts.

I should never have bought the new pair if it had not been for the small boy in charge of the store. It was on the main street, about three blocks from the hotel, and it was a little store of the kind that calls itself a Mammoth Emporium. I happened to look into the window in passing, and something incredibly red caught my eye. I could not be sure what it was, and so I went into the store, and it was a small boy's head bent down over a paper-covered book. He looked up as I came in, and on the spur of the moment I bought the boots. They were the best boots I ever bought. I have them now and they are still in fine fettle. They profess to be made of elk-skin and I have no doubt they are — and they cost me two dollars and seventy-five cents.

The weather was glorious and the country was charming and I didn't feel like doing any work and I just loafed around. About two days after I bought the new shoes I began to realise that I was the object of universal, though quite respectful, interest. I found it impossible to be alone, wherever I went. If I was in a place that no one else had visited since the days of Captain Kidd, I might be sure that, after I had been there ten minutes, I should run across a whole band of aborigines — most of them young — trying their very hardest to look as if they had foregathered by accident and without the remotest idea of finding me there. It became embarrassing at last and I began to think of going back to New York. Then, one evening, an elderly gentleman called at the hotel and sent in his name to me, and said that he had been robbed of six couple, or brace, or pair, whichever is the technical term, of his prize strain of Buff Orpingtons, and was I ready to take up the case?

I discovered then that I was a famous detective, or "sleuth," disguised, for professional reasons, as an English vagabond. There had been a burglary at a country-place near Amicus and I had been sent for from New York to trail down the burglars; and that was why I was lounging around Amicus, seeming to do nothing, but all the while stretching my stupendous brain and my super-eagle eye to their uttermost. My red-headed young friend in the shoe-store was the first to discover me. He was a fervent student of the works of that greatest of all great "sleuths," Mr. Nick Carter, whose multitudinous exploits, recounted in I know not how many hundreds or thousands of little paper-covered books at fifteen cents each, have made him one of the most deservedly popular figures of the Western Continent. I have read hundreds of his adventures myself. At one time I had a perfect passion for them and used to buy them by the half-dozen, at a reduced price after he had read them himself, from a news storekeeper on Sixth Avenue.

The red-headed boy, overwhelmed by the spectacle of a total stranger to Amicus buying a pair of shoes at two dollars and seventy-five cents, very naturally set his wits to work along the lines suggested by his favourite hero and, as naturally, decided, from the vacuity of my countenance, that I must be a disguised detective. I am inclined to think and to be flattered by the thought that he took me for Mr. Carter himself, from the respect, almost amounting to veneration, with which I was treated by the youth of Amicus. I am inclined to fear also, that he lost, or imperilled, his situation in the shoe-store world, for, wherever and under whatever circumstances I might become aware of my respectful circle of admirers, there you might be sure, blazing in the van, like the white plume of King Henry, was the scarlet poll I came to know so well. I think he hoped that I might some day give him a position in the ranks of my assistants; I have not the least doubt in the world that he it was who spread my fame in Amicus.

I was sorely tempted to accept the task of trailing the lost Buff Orpingtons to their lair, but respect for the character of the distinguished gentleman I was representing, who I was sure would never have accepted a commission so trivial, led me to refuse. Instead, I came next morning to an understanding with my host, wherein I assured him that I was no sleuth but a simple vagabond on the look-out for a job, and that I should greatly value his assistance in finding one.

I believe, although he spoke no word, that he was bitterly disappointed. I know that he was perturbed, because he three times went towards the window and studied his clue without once pausing to sit down on the bed-edge. Still without speaking, he left the room and I saw no more of him that day. Without any real reason I felt as remorseful as though I had intentionally deceived him, and sooner than face his reproachful silence I decided to leave Amicus that evening. In the end I put it off until the next morning and I was glad of it. In the first place I received an anonymous letter, which I still preserve for guidance when I bring out my long-projected Spelling Primer. It was addressed to " Nick Carter or Chick or Patsy Sleuth." It was written in red ink and sealed, so to put it, with the representation of a blood-red hand holding a scarlet dagger, from which dripped very realistic drops of gore. It ran as follows: "You are none bewair the red hand is upon your trale iff you would escap yore liffe mete me disgusd cor. First and Vale Av at midnite i will gide too a place of safety a frind who meanes you well."

It was written in an appropriately unformed hand, girlish I am inclined to think, rather than boyish and I was delighted to receive it, if only that it proved that Young England and Young America are united by bonds stronger than could be forged by many arbitration treaties.

I have been sorry ever since that it did not at the time enter my head to keep the appointment. I can only hope that any disappointment I unwittingly caused was more than outweighed by the undoubted fact that I left my hotel next morning; sufficient proof, I hope, to the friend who meant me well that his (or her) warning had been treated with proper respect.

I was compelled to leave, quite against my will and almost under physical compulsion. Mine host turned up at my bedside at his usual hour, in a state of high excitement, which he showed by adding to his expected headline (on that occasion, "Clam Beach. Gustave Olaffson. Lost his help.") something about a boat. Thereafter he rushed to the window, consulted his clue, returned at racing pace and uttered the further command, "Come right now." He then departed without further words, but he left me so disturbed by his portentous loquacity that I rose at once, to find him awaiting me at the stair-foot, as though he feared I might otherwise escape him. He allowed me but little time for my breakfast; and then, hooking his arm in mine, led me away with him as might Mr. Carter a defaulting cashier.

Thus personally conducted I arrived some half-hour later, before a little wooden shanty on Clam Beach. Clam Beach itself was a kind of holiday annexe to Amicus — a tiny settlement on the long, sandy barrier reef that guards the southern shores of Long Island. There were perhaps twenty wooden bungalows and a ramshackle hotel, and Mr. Olaffson's bathing establishment; and they were all connected, like captured flies on a cobweb, by single planks across the sand-dunes. You got to it from Amicus by a crazy old motor-launch across the shallowest, clearest of lagoons.

Mr. Olaffson's establishment was set on a sand-dune midway between the Ocean and the lagoon. It is a curious fact, by the way, that what is referred to as the sea in England is always known in America as the Ocean. It is just the same old Atlantic at Long Island as it is at the Land's End, but when an American talks about it you can see it swelling itself out with pride and bridling with pleasure. It is the same with most natural things somehow. If you took an English hill over to America, and set it down all small and humble-minded in a field, by the time it woke up next morning it would be a Mountain, with all the appropriate airs and graces, boasting of its cousins the Rockies and speaking pityingly of the Himalayas because, being Asiatics, they can never become naturalised American citizens. I have been told, though I do not vouch for it, that when the moon — the same old moon that we have in England — looks down on America she calls herself a Planet and not a satellite at all. It has something to do with the atmosphere, I suppose.

Mr. Olaffson was a very, very old man and he really wanted a help or, as we should say, an assistant. He was much too old to do anything but sit outside his castle in the sunlight, smoking and cursing under his breath. I say cursing, because it sounded like it, though he was really a very amiable person, and we got on famously. Out of the kindness of his heart my friend Mr. Godly assured him that I spoke Swedish perfectly. It was a safe enough assertion because, although Mr. Olaffson was a Swede all right, he had been in America so many centuries that he had quite forgotten Swedish. He had never succeeded in learning more than three words of American either, and he could not master the meaning even of them. So we used to communicate by signs.

The Castle, as I called it — a name which I am told it has ever since retained — was a wooden building that was a cross between a barn and a mediæval gate-house. There was a big room on top, where bathing suits and towels and things were stored, and a little one below on each side where Mr. Olaffson and I slept, and another big one in the middle that was more a corridor than a room, with a huge door at either end. Through it you reached the bathing-boxes. They stood round a yard or compound and they were arranged in the shape of a big M, one wing for women and the other for men. The boxes themselves were about the size and shape of roomy coffins, with a little seat inside, and besides being bathing-boxes they acted as incubators for sand-flies. I believe myself that all the sand-flies of Long Island looked upon our compound as their terrestrial Paradise. They used to settle there in millions and bring up their families and wait for visitors. It was very shrewd of them, because, by the time a bather was undressed, the superficial area of their food-supply was increased I don't know how many fold, compared with what it was either before he got out of his ordinary clothes or after he was in his bathing-suit. Evidently, too, they liked the flavour of women better than men, perhaps because they smoke less, for there were always three times as many in the women's wing and they looked healthier and bit more blithely.

Although Clam Beach was a delightful place in its way and the bathing glorious, it was not the kind of work I really cared about, and I should never have taken it on but that I hated the thought of hurting Mr. Godly's feelings. There has been always something repulsive to me in the feel of a dank, cold, limp bathing-suit after it has been used and is all covered with sand. When I had to deal with dozens and dozens of them, they grew more and more repulsive, and I got to feel like a rheumatic ghoul condemned to work in a damp cemetery. Mr. Olaffson's company was not inspiring either. The visitors were always nice enough to me and their ideas about tips compared more than favourably with those prevalent in English sea-side resorts, and if I had stopped on I might have had a castle of my own by this time. But the heat of the summer was waning and I felt the call of the city again, and one morning I ran away and took the first train back to New York. I felt I couldn't face Mr. Godly, so I sent him a message to say I had been called away on urgent business and that someday I was coming back again. I am going, too, whenever I get the chance, because I have nothing but pleasant memories of Amicus and there are very few places of which I can say that.

CHAPTER XII

"Seeing New York"

THE millionaire baby, before and after birth, is an important asset to the social life of New York. I do not mean only to people in the same station of life to which he has been called, but to quite a lot of low vulgar common folk, myself among them. Three — or it may have been four — millionaire babies — two of them unborn — provided me with two solid weeks of lucrative work on my return from Amicus, and it was only through my ungrateful neglect of them that I lost it.

As I walked out of the Pennsylvania Terminus I suddenly realised that I was the victim of a bad attack of ambition. For one thing, I had over twenty dollars in my pocket; for another, I had quite a presentable suit of clothes

— so long as I stood in the shadow and hid my knees and my shoulder-blades behind something. I bought the suit second-hand when I was a Hindu magician, and the vendor assured me that he could guarantee it, as he had worn it for five years and it had never flinched.

I took a hall-room on West Forty-fourth Street, and by some marvellous good luck the coloured lady who answered the door, when she felt like it, was rather struck by me — and I escaped having to pay a deposit beforehand. I was rather struck by the coloured lady, too — especially when she supposed I was English, made a casual remark about " damn Yankees," and told me she was English herself. She said that children of the Empire on which the sun never sets should stand shoulder to shoulder. She asked me if I came from London, and, when I said I did, she rather thought we might be cousins, because she was born in Brixton herself. As a matter of fact, I had washed quite hard that morning, but I only said it was very likely indeed.

It was through Cousin Euphemia that I became a guide-lecturer. It was quite by accident, too; if I had had enough money left at the end of the third week to pay my bill, I should very likely be looking for work now. I tried hard to get a clerkship or something that would live up to my clothes, but I don't suppose I went the right way about it. I answered advertisements, but somehow, as soon as I had found the place and screwed up my courage to go in and ask about the job, I used to get turned out. I don't mean physically. I used to be taken into a room where there was a wooden desk and a man sitting behind it with a face that had been carved out of the same piece of wood. Before I could say anything he would look at me and say, "Nop," and go on with what he was doing. It never varied. In the end I got desperate, and I went to one of the big office-buildings on Broadway and I tried every office in it. There was always the same man and the same desk, and he always looked at me and said, "Nop"— all the way down from the eighteenth floor to the ground. After that I lost interest and went down to the

Battery and watched the liners on their way to England.

At the end of the third week I only had two dollars towards the five I owed. I told Cousin Euphemia about it, and she suggested that I should be a guide-lecturer. She told me of a firm on Broadway, and I got a recommendation from my friend Dempsey, the policeman, in which he very kindly said I was his brother, and so I got the job. I used to drive about on a motor *char-à-banc,* a long, sloping arrangement like those you see in London in the summer. I had a megaphone and explained the sights in a loud voice. New York isn't half a bad place, but it is deficient in sights, and if it wasn't for the millionaire babies I am afraid I should have sometimes had to invent things. Fortunately, though, the country tripper who comes to New York doesn't care about sights as we understand them in England — unless they are very expensive. My most popular tour used to start by passing the Waldorf Hotel. We used to stop there while I told them what was the annual income of the guests who put up there, and how much the ladies in the Peacock Parade spent on diamonds for their shoe-heels, and that sort of thing. I am no good at figures, and I expect they varied sometimes, but my clients were always satisfied. Then we used to take them to Saint Patrick's Cathedral. They didn't trouble to go inside, of course, but we stopped for a minute or two while I told them what the site cost, and the average value of the jewels in the copes and things worn by the clergy. Then we went on up Fifth Avenue to where the babies lived. Luckily for me there was quite a glut of them at that time. When we passed a likely looking house — you can always tell, because millionaire architecture reminds you of a new restaurant in Leicester Square — we used to pull up while I explained, through the megaphone, that we were opposite the princely home of Mr. Potiphar J. Scrawlenfeldt, whose income was so many millions a week, and who had spent so many billions on the house and so many on the furniture, and had married the daughter of so many more, and

I had a megaphone and explained the sights in a loud voice.

was expecting a son in about three weeks, who would be heir to so many trillions. I was rather successful.

We weren't the only sightseers by any means. Sometimes there would be half-a-dozen cars at once, stopping opposite one mansion, each with a megaphone going, which made things cheerful for the expectant mother. If I had been her I think I should have felt embarrassed, but in New York she gets to look for it, and sometimes she would appear at a window by accident amid the cheers of the rubberers, and the booming of the megaphones, and the clicking of the living-picture cameras. As I said, I was rather successful and I am not at all sure that I had not really found my occupation in life if only my success hadn't resulted in a bad attack of swelled head. There is one bit of Manhattan where there really are some sights, as we of the old world understand them. Between Wall Street — where the old wall stood in the Dutch days — and the nose of the island there are a lot of quaint streets and one or two old houses — seventeenth-century sort of style — with a certain amount of old-world feeling about them that, in my insular prejudice, I thought would make up a good lecture. I got my proprietor to try sending a car round there for a change, and rashly guaranteed that I could make a success of it. I couldn't. On my fourth trip I only had two rubberers, and they were both furious because I didn't show them where the Bilkheimer baby was expected. They complained when we got back. The boss told me I was too intellectual — only he didn't put it quite so nicely — and I had to leave.

CHAPTER XIII

A Turn at Starving

IF we had always to eat the same food I suppose we should never eat anything. I know at least that quite the worst aspect of starvation is its monotony; there is nothing else anywhere that can equal it in lack of incident. After I lost my job as a guide-lecturer I had a run of really bad luck, and I learnt the whole philosophy of starvation at first hand. I was not a bit well, to start with. If I had been moving in a more exalted sphere I suppose I should have said I had a nervous breakdown. As it was, I could only call it an absolute lack of energy, or moral force, or something of that sort, that gave me an infinite distaste for doing anything at all. Unkind people might call it sheer laziness; but it was not that. On the contrary, I used to have terrific fits of energy; but they always tailed away just at the moment when they began to produce results. I used to spend hours working out great schemes towards this, that or the other mighty end, and then dropping them. Very naturally they none of them came to anything and I came to real starvation.

There is only one good thing about starving; the longer it lasts the less it hurts. The first day is the worst — because your mind feels it most. If ever I wanted to start a Terror, I should pick only men who had starved absolutely for twenty-four hours. After that you begin to lose interest.

I had to leave my hall-room — which corresponds to an attic in London, though it is really a little room fitted in over the entrance hall — after the first week. I left it with thirty-five cents in my pocket and the well-wishes of my coloured cousin Euphemia. I husbanded my fortune, but it did not last long; New York is an expensive city. I couldn't get a job; I knew nobody who could help me towards one; even my friend Dempsey was absent from his usual beat. I was absurdly ignorant about charities. They exist, of course, by dozens, but I didn't know of them. If any one who reads this wants to start a charity, let him establish one for strangers, without regard to their deserts, and let him advertise its whereabouts by huge posters, so that any poor devil can find it. He mustn't ask any questions either. I have no doubt a native New Yorker — as, in London, a native Londoner — would know exactly where to find a free meal and have a dozen excellent reasons for getting it. I didn't, and there are many thousands like me. While I had sufficient energy left to inquire, I had sufficient to look for a job, and when that was gone I was past inquiring. I did have some vague idea of appealing to the British Consul. I even went to look for him, but when I found the place — down by the Battery, at the corner of Whitehall Street, I think it is — it was so shabby and had so dirty an entrance that I didn't go in. This sounds absurd enough, but it is true. That was the third day of my fast, and I suppose I was getting fanciful.

The first day, as I say, my mind suffered most. I stormed and raved inwardly at every one who looked as if he had enough money on him for the next meal. The second day my body suffered. I had the most horrible indigestion sort of cramps — exactly as if I had eaten too much. I remember thinking how unfair it was. The third day both mind and body suffered, only less acutely. I was fool enough to eat something on the fourth. A bench neighbour — a working man who had got drunk over night and had a black eye, and was afraid to go home and face his wife — gave me a quarter, and I spent twenty cents of it on food, most of it on corned (or, as we should say, salt) beef hash. It made me quite horribly ill — until I was mercifully sick, after which I felt better. I spent the remaining five cents upon cigarettes — they were called "Hassans,"— ten of them. I don't know who made them, but here is an unsolicited testimonial: I never enjoyed anything so much in my life. Like a fool, I smoked them all right off on end, with no thought for the morrow, and I felt uncommonly ill afterwards for the second time. I was beyond caring about things much.

Past the Battery Park, at the very nose of the island of Manhattan, are the big termini from which the ferry boats start for Brooklyn and Staten Island and other suburbs. There is an iron gallery beside one of them, approached by a long flight of steps, where you can stand and watch all the shipping coming up and down the harbour. I found it out by accident, the day I was looking for the Consulate — and I got into the way of going there and watching out for ships that flew the Union Jack. There were three of them to one of any other flag, and somehow it did me a lot of good. I felt quite a ridiculous amount of pride in the thought that there was still something in the world in which I had some little share. I expect I should have pawned my share just then if it had had any cash value, but the feeling was there all the same.

On the sixth day I was feeling thoroughly content — in a sort of dreamy haze in which nothing mattered in all this world or the next. I slept on a bench in the Battery Park. It rained a little and I got wet, but was too lazy to move in under the shelter of the Elevated, and I saw the *Olympic,* I think it was, going out, and followed her with my eyes all the way until she got lost in the mist somewhere by Staten Island, and gloried to myself that she was the biggest boat in the world and English. Then I took it into my head to walk round the path between the little park and the water's edge, where the excursion steamers start. It was about ten o'clock in the morning.

The excursion boats are very popular in the warm weather, and there is a good deal of competition among them, and they all have runners out to catch the unwary tripper who hasn't quite made up his mind. I was mooning along, thinking about nothing at all, when there came a little spirtle of wind from the water and something slapped me across the eyes. I grabbed at it, and it was a dollar bill. I saw then that it must have come from one of the ticket touts, who stand about with tickets in one hand, ready to sell, and bunches of dollars in the other, to show what good business they are doing and how popular their boats are.

I suppose if I had thought about it I should have stuck to that greenback, but the habit of instinctive honesty is difficult to throw off. Anyway, I took it to its proper owner. He was a large red Jew, but a white man all the same. I must have looked like a second-class pirate; I hadn't shaved or washed, or had my clothes off, for a week, and I think I was a bit unsteady in my walk by that time. But either he was amazed at my honesty or he saw I looked rather faded; anyhow, he took me in and did for me. He made me sit down on a bench and wait until he was off duty, and then he stood me a meal — a sensible meal, only hot soup to begin with — and a wash and a shave. And, by the way, whoever starts my ideal stranger's charity should provide it with free baths and washing accommodation and free shaving. How any man who looks as I did, dirty and ragged, and with a week-old beard on his face, and the smell — for even the cleanest of us are unpleasant after we have worn our clothes for a week consecutively — how he can be expected to find work, or to have the heart to look for it, is past my comprehension. There ought to be free collars and cuffs provided, too, even if they are only made of paper; nothing improves a man's chances so much as wearing a clean collar. The coat doesn't matter nearly so much.

To make a long story short, my Jewish friend got me a berth on the Lake Island boats — as I will call them — to go round among the passengers and take orders for beer. Afterwards, when a vacancy fell in, I might look forward to acting as bar-man in a curious little horseshoe bar tucked away between the paddle-wheels. I had a white coat and a clean face, and I bought myself a dandy yachting cap, and altogether if I had met myself of a week before I shouldn't have cared to be seen speaking to me. That was the worst week I spent in New York, and I don't want another like it anywhere.

CHAPTER XIV

The Child Terrible

I SOMETIMES wonder whether London or New York has most to complain of, in the way of reputation. If you believe the accounts of the untravelled American, who has not been there, London is a chaotic dust-heap, only rendered tolerable by the fact that constant fogs prevent your seeing it. New York again is revealed to the unseeing eyes of the English world as a wilderness of impossibly tall skyscrapers, divided up into exactly regular blocks, and peopled by hurrying hordes who dash madly about rectilinearly, overturning each other without shame in the race for wealth.

As a matter of fact, except for a few outlying examples, the skyscrapers of New York are all bunched up together in a space very much smaller than the One Square Mile, and the rest of the city is a cross between Bloomsbury and Berlin. So much for the works of Man; Nature has given it a setting so gracious that not all mankind working for eternity will ever be able to make it anything less than beautiful. And its greatest beauties are concentrated about its waterways. The best way to see New York is by steamer and the only drawback is that in that case you can scarcely avoid the huge advertisement sign, set out in enormous letters in front of Brooklyn, which tells you that a certain Hungarian mineral water is invaluable for stomachic complaints. I have bowdlerised it considerably, but such is its general message. It is at least as blatant to the eye of incoming steamship passengers as is the statue of Liberty. I do not say that it is out of place. Liberty and stomachic complaints are certainly the keynotes of American life; and whoever arranged that the Liberty Statue should stand with her back to America, looking towards Europe with a hopeful expression, as though watching out for a really reliable liver-pill, knew his country.

As has been said of Manchester, one of the best features of New York is the ease with which you can get away from it. It has a service of excursion steamers to everywhere that could not be bettered anywhere in the world, despite a tendency to explode at odd moments. You can go by steamer to I know not how many ports and towns and pleasure resorts at whatever distance you prefer; you can go for very little indeed, and you may be sure that wherever you go you will thoroughly enjoy the voyage.

The steamer on which I sold beer for a time was called, let us say, the *Jane McCracken,* and plied between the Battery and Lake Island, which is a pleasant summer resort in the State of New York, about thirty miles by water from the City, and looking over the Sound which divides Long Island from the continent. It is a very popular voyage and very rightly, for even I, who had to make the trip twice a day in the way of duty, enjoyed it thoroughly, embarrassed though I was by a tray of ice-cream cornucopias, a collection of beer-glasses, or a load of pop-corn, according to circumstances.

I know no better way of getting acquainted with a people than by studying them at their pleasures, and I would defy any one to study the New York populace, as exemplified by travellers on the Lake Island Line, without liking them. They were not so well disciplined, in the way of queues and crowding, as would be, say, a Bank Holiday mob in London; they were at least as kindly and very much more sociable. Thanks, I suppose, to the large proportion of Jews among them, the Lake Island trippers were more patriarchally gregarious than are the Londoners. I do not mean to say that there was not a fair percentage of detached couples; but for the most part they tripped in family batches, grandfather and grandmother, father and mother, four assorted aunts and uncles, and, say, three hobbledehoys and as many flappers — or, as New York has it, "broilers"— each provided with an appropriate sweetheart, and courting under the maternal eye with a determined earnestness only to be equalled by the couples on the benches in Hyde Park of a Sunday evening. Then, of course, there were the children — shoals of them. Professionally speaking, the children were the most welcome of all our patrons, in that they had an insatiable appetite for ice-cream, which I vended, arranged in little cornucopias of wafer at five cents each. Their elders, on the other hand, not infrequently brought their own viands, and were as such less desirable, seeing that I was partly paid by a percentage on the receipts.

We were not, of course, confined to tripper traffic. We had a large number of regular passengers, living in and around New Rochelle and similar suburban centres, who used our boat as the pleasantest link with New York. Some of them I got to know very well, and especially Helga, who was at once the wickedest and the most fascinating little minx I ever knew.

Actually I know very little about her, as she

would vary her information about herself according to her mood of the moment. I call her Helga because such was the first name she mentioned to me, but she called herself by quite a number of others, according as she thought them momentarily desirable. So with her age; at different times she told me that she was five, seven, eight, nine, ten and even once, sixteen, which I did not believe. She was an uncommonly pretty monkey with a fresh little face, full of deviltry, a mop of golden hair, and very long, slim, black legs, which were I think her most characteristic feature. She made love to me most scandalously, from the first time that she saw me with my ice-cream tray; and thereafter whenever she was aboard paid me, or it, unending breathless court. She had an exceedingly comfortable-looking papa and a very pretty mamma, whom I used to observe gazing at her with languid surprise as though wondering how she could be responsible for such a bantling. She would refer to her father in casual conversation as "the Man" and considerably embarrassed me, upon our second meeting, by leading me, tray and all, up to her mother and demanding loudly, " Isn't she perfectly sweet? "

I mention her with some particularity, firstly because I fell desperately in love with her, and secondly because she was, directly, the cause of my very narrowly escaping drowning and, indirectly, of my losing my employment. At Lake Island, our terminus, the boat used to be made fast to an ornamental pier-head in a tiny bay, into and out of which it had to back with unusual care. On one occasion while it was backing towards the pier I happened to be standing beside the Monkey on a little platform just abaft the paddle-box. In the usual way it was protected by an iron railing, but that had been removed, in readiness for landing. The Monkey, whose chief joy was to arouse her seniors' fears by pushing herself into dangerous positions, managed in some way to drop overboard a large model of a torpedo-boat with which her father had that day dowered her. I daresay it was an excellent model, but it was no swimmer and promptly disappeared in the foam from the starboard paddle. About to burst into a scream of anguish, the Monkey, presuming as usual, upon my devotion, changed her mind and ordered me, with her most fascinating *moue,* to jump overboard after it. I declined. Thereupon, with the calm remark, "Then perhaps you will jump after *me,*" she promptly leapt after her toy into the water. Drowning is a death after which I have no sort of hankering and I was about to turn on my heel, in order to acquaint the captain with the loss of one of his passengers, when my foot somehow slipped and I followed her. Once in the water there seemed no particular reason why I should not so far assist the imp as to guide her away from the paddle-blades, which were twirling about in the air just over and unpleasantly close to our heads. I have an impression that the water was not more than three or four feet deep. However that may be, we scrambled ashore, without damage, except to my temper, in about a minute; whereafter ensued a scene of which I cannot think even now, without a blush of reminiscent shame. There happened to be a clergyman on board and a reporter — it would be amazing if there had not been, in a country where both are so common — and I will not dwell upon the horrid orgy that ensued. I did not see most of it, because I was engaged in borrowing dry clothes from the rest of the crew, but by the time I got on deck again the clergyman had arrived at Fourthly; and the reporter, having interviewed all the passengers, the crew and the pier officials, was discussing with the captain the possibility of having the affair re-enacted before the cinematograph machine he proposed to rush down from New York by automobile.

You will understand that there was only one thing to be done. My borrowed plumes fortunately proved sufficient disguise; a trolley-car was about to start on the other side of the ferry; in half-an-hour I was in New Rochelle and in another ninety minutes or so I was back in New York, a workless wanderer once more. I cannot say how sorry I was. I was quite absurdly fond of the Monkey, and apart from her,

I was very happy on the *Jane McCracken.* I have knocked about the world a good deal in my time, but I do not know when I have seen anything more beautiful than some of the trips we used to make homewards after sunset, down the Sound. It is an enchanted shore at the worst of times — something like the trip up to Southampton from the Needles, only five times as long and, especially after sundown, a dozen times as beautiful. There is always a mysterious shore to right and left, fading and advancing as you turn and twist along the channel. Just as you start you will have the melting gold and russet and saffron of the sunset, deepening into violet, on your right hand; and suddenly behind you the whole of Lake Island bursts into a luminous outline of little points of fire, as they turn on the illuminations. They are only electric lights and they outline quite ugly things, a Ferris Wheel and a mountain railway and so on, but as you leave them behind they twist themselves into pagodas and enchanted palaces and vague dancing shapes that are too elusive to build thoughts upon, or more than visions. The Sound is very still, only a soft fresh breeze fans your temples and all around you the pale shadows of the islands deepen to purple invisibility; and somewhere ahead are the blood-red and flowery green pin-pricks of passing vessels; and little bustling lights spring out on the growing shores and behind you the glimmer of the golden palaces of fairyland fades and fades. Everything seems hushed and stilled into eternal immobility; you only are rushing through space on the wings of the night; somewhere above you, waving solemnly across the starlight, are the great propeller beams that make the *Jane McCracken* seem like a sluggish spider drawing itself along an unseen web. The lights of Lake Island fade at last into a mere incandescence behind you, and other stars rise slowly from the unseen distances you go to meet. To sit there, on the upper deck, with the woman you love and gaze out forward, to where one solitary golden star set high in the heavens tells you — although it is in itself nothing more romantic than the clock-face of the Metropolitan Life Building in Madison Square a dozen miles away from you — that somewhere the only real Paradise — they call it Home — is waiting . . .

But this is all very absurd, well enough for married, respectable folk, lords and slaves of small imps with warm, confiding palms, but not for vagabonds, with no more useful mission in life than to take orders for beer. "Ice-cream! Ice-cream!! Now then, Folks — who wants ice-cream? Five cents! Only Five Cents!"

CHAPTER XV

Called to the Bar

I ATTAINED the summit of human ambition — as understood by many millions of people in New York, London, and elsewhere — on the same day that I became a life-long teetotaller from birth, like Mr. Bryan, Mr. Lloyd George and other notabilities. I do not mean because of it. It happened after I had dismissed myself from my job on the *Jane McCracken.* I had to visit her, in secret, in order to give back the clothes I had borrowed and to collect what was left of my own. They were not unshrinkable, unfortunately, and there was very little of them left.

I am inclined to think that the most remarkable thing about humanity is the number of really nice people — white men, as you would say in America — it includes. In my erratic wanderings through life the preponderance of white folk I have come across is quite overwhelming; it is true that, judged by the ordinary standards of morality, some of them might be regarded, by respectable people, as very rank outsiders indeed. I am reminded of this when I think of Captain — technically known as " Cap "— Lane, who was the skipper of the *Jane McCracken.* I have heard it darkly hinted, among the crew — a crew, be it remembered, is at least as devoted to scandal as is a convent or a small provincial town — that " Cap " Lane was a most immoral man — that, exceeding the proverbial privilege accorded to sea-faring men, he not only had a wife in every port, but two or three. If so, I am sure they were all devoted to him, and that however many children he may have had, he was an ideal father to each and all of them. He was rather a small man, with a bluff voice that yet had in it the sort of timbre that made you want to put your head on his shoulder and sob out your troubles to him. I never did, because my relations with him were purely official, but if I had been his wife, or somebody else's, I can imagine myself doing it all day long. He was just coming off the *Jane McCracken* when I met him.

Cap Lane used to drink a great deal more than was good for him. He drank according to a system of his own. For twenty-two hours out of the twenty-four he was strictly teetotal. I think it was the result of some promise he had made to his mother on her death-bed, but anyway he had to crowd into two hours all the drinking that the ordinary man can spread through the day and part of the night. He was very methodical about it. Our last trip usually brought us back to New York somewhere after nine in the evening. As soon as the ship was moored Cap Lane left her at once, betook himself to a saloon on Greenwich Street, and set himself solidly to the task of pouring into himself as much liquor as was humanly possible in the short one hundred and twenty minutes available. I do not believe he liked it — not, at least, taken at railway speed;

he regarded it as a stern duty and he did. I do not think it ever made him drunk. On at least one occasion I was privileged to see him home — to one of his homes at any rate, in Greenwich. He was certainly not drunk then; he explained to me, I remember, the method in which pilots "con" a ship and he did it as clearly as might a mathematical professor. Yet, as it was currently reported, he already carried within himself that evening enough liquor to enable a moderate-sized steamer to come to her moorings without any fear of grounding whatever.

I met him, as I say, just as I was slinking towards the gangway, in the faint hope that I might secure my small property without attracting undue attention. He captured me, in silence, and drew me with him across the park and into the saloon of his choice. There, fixing me with his eye, he held me in irons until he had produced from his pocket a letter. It was from Helga's father and it was quite flattering — evidently the Monkey had held fast to her self-imposed convention of never telling the truth where a lie was possible — and it enclosed a hundred-dollar bill.

One of the commonest mistakes made by people of the middle and upper-middle classes is to suppose that they and their superiors monopolise the finer shades of sensibility. Cap Lane was not "*geboren*," as the Germans have it. He first saw the light in the cabin of a barge on the Erie Canal, and spent most of his youth irritating with a bent pin at the end of a stick the tails of the mules who drew his father and his fortunes. Yet he understood at once why I did not feel like taking that hundred-dollar bill, and he agreed to divide the reward among the members of the crew and their auxiliaries and did it faithfully. What is more, he carried me off with him, that same evening, to the saloon on Eighth Avenue owned by a friend named Macgregor. Mr. Macgregor had all the assistants he required, but that made no difference at all. He had to accept me — and knowing Cap Lane I suppose he knew it; and within five minutes I was setting up the bottles and the Cap was pouring chasers down his throat; and I can honestly say that I was not nearly so clumsy as you would have thought at the time, but that I really was trying to help him go slow.

What we call a public-house, and usually believe that the Americans call a saloon, calls itself in New York a café — or as an American Pitman would spell it, a kaafe. When I became a bar-tender in a café I had to become a lifelong teetotaller from birth, because that is almost a *sine qua non* in New York bar-tending. At the same time I was raised in the public eye to a rank a little higher than a marquisate in England and a little lower than a dukedom.

The bar-tender is the only person in New York who is addressed as "sir"— in the English way of using the word — by what we should call the lower classes. The policeman is sometimes similarly honoured by uninstructed foreigners, but only when they are honest. The rest, who are in the majority, call him "son" or "youse guy," according to the closeness of their intimacy. The bar-tender — and especially the proprietor — is not at all the pimply, dirty old Irish reprobate with an impossible brogue, a hard-worked sense of humour and an unquenchable loquacity, popularised by Mr. Dooley and other humorists. Instead, he is a silent, keen-eyed, close-lipped business man, with a neat taste in tailoring and a prejudice against alcoholic stimulant. I have said I was a teetotaller; so were my three colleagues, and the boy and the terrier and the proprietor — some of even longer standing. Two were earnest church workers — Scotch Presbyterians, as well — but I was not, because it was optional.

You need a character if you wish to prosper as a New York bar-tender. In some other trades — politics and the delicatessen industry, for instance — you are better without one. Instead, in applying for a job, if the boss — pronounced "baws," by the way — asks if you have had experience, you say nothing at all — you just wink and smile. The more meaning you can get into that wink the more certain you are of getting the job. I had a character — given me by Cap Lane, and he knew the boss's prejudices. The boss's name was, as I have said, Macgregor, and he was from County Down, and had a liking for his fellow-countrymen. So I was from County Down, too, like the rest of the establishment, down to the terrier. My name was Mackintosh — with the accent on the I — but I left home very young before I learned to speak Ulster, as my father was an earnest Orangeman, much persecuted by the local Papistry. I was born in a village, the name of which I forget, but which Mr. Macgregor recognised as soon as Cap Lane told him of it, though he had not visited it for some years. He was able to tell me all about it, and even to describe the cottage I must have been born in. After a time he began to remember my father and what a decent man he was, and how he had a son who used to go about in a hat three sizes too large for him. I said it was my elder brother, but he insisted it was I, because he began to remember the boy's face, and it had exactly my eyes and hair and nose, and was inclined to stoutness. We nearly quarrelled over it, and I found out he was an ill man to contradict. He insisted on calling me Alexander afterwards, which was the elder brother's name, instead of William, which was mine, because he was quite sure I *was* the elder brother, who had got into trouble for shooting at a parish priest from behind a hedge, and was trying to pass myself off as my own junior. It was a bit mixed, but it made us very good friends again, and he promised to put me up for the "martyr" branch of his Lodge, which included all those who had suffered for the Cause.

The café was on the corner of a block, as most of them are. Nearly every block in New York has a café at each of its four corners, a couple of gambling-hells somewhere handy, eight shoe-shining stands, where they also sell oranges and chocolates, and a church. I don't say this is universal; sometimes one of the shoe-shining stands is left out and sometimes the church, but never the cafés. They are rather like churches themselves in atmosphere. Ours was, at any rate. I suggested, when I had been there some little time, that it would not be a bad idea to open proceedings with prayer, according to the ritual of the Church of Scotland. I meant it humorously, but Mr. Macgregor was struck with the idea, and only gave it up for fear it would be bad for the business, as we had so many Jewish customers. He liked me all the better for it, though.

Curiously enough, one of our customers was Mr. Cholmondely, whose delicatessen store was only a few blocks off. As you may remember, we had parted unfriends on a matter of chickens. So the first evening he came in when I was serving, feeling rather proud of my white coat and white apron — white suits my complexion, I have been told — I made up my mind to ignore him. He wouldn't be ignored, though; he reached out for my hand as if it had been a greenback, and stood there slobbering with his hat off and calling me "Ma tear," and waiting with a pathetic little smile for me to nod to him. I realised then for the first time how high I had risen.

When I say the café was like a church, I mean that you never heard loud voices or bad language in it. Customers all had a deferential air, and used to swallow their whisky — always " chasers," whisky first and water afterwards out of two separate glasses — as if it was medicine. The place was all swathed in white muslin, with pink rosettes, to keep the flies off the looking-glasses, and the bar was a big round horseshoe, like a rostrum, swept and garnished, and behind it was a sort of trophy of bottles like an organ-case. All this decency and propriety was because there were no barmaids and no women customers. None visible, I mean. I have often heard good Americans lament over the number of women you see in public-houses in London, and rejoice that such a spectacle is unknown in New York. That is because they know nothing of the " Family Entrance." There aren't " public " and " private " and " saloon " bars in New York, but there *is* a family entrance, which in our case meant a little room at the back of the café with a separate door. It was used chiefly on Sundays when we were supposed to be shut, and there would be more women than men in it half the time. It was used after closing hours, too. We nominally closed at one, by which time the really seasoned topers hadn't got properly to work, but we kept open as long as there were any customers. Because I was rather large and heavy Macgregor put me on duty in the "Family" department right from the beginning, and there was not any ecclesiastical atmosphere about that. Chucking out was not so easy as it is in London, because every café has storm doors — glass-porch arrangements to keep out the cold in winter — and if your man struggled it was difficult to get him through without breaking the glass. Macgregor was in favour of stunning him first, but if you killed him you were almost certain to have trouble with the police and get fined or something.

I stayed at the café quite a long time; and I only left because I was offered a partnership by a customer in vaudeville, which had always interested me.

CHAPTER XVI

A Son of the Empire

THE educational value of the public-house is seldom recognised by social reformers. In actual fact it has all the advantages of that academy to which the elder Mr. Weller sent his son Samuel, with none of its drawbacks. Personally, I learned more in Mr. Macgregor's café than I have ever learned outside it — and not of matters connected with the liquor trade only. For one thing, I learned to understand English.

When I first went to New York I got a job on a newspaper. I am ashamed to say how short a time I held it, and I cannot fairly quarrel with the reason for my dismissal, which was that my English was very much too provincial for a really high-toned metropolitan journal. More urgent matters prevented my giving any appreciable time to the study of the language until I became a bar-tender, and then I realised how thoroughly justified had been my expulsion from that first newspaper office. But I did not despair. I set to work to master the subject, and by the time I had learned the four chief secrets I felt emboldened to try my prentice hand at journalism once more. I do not mean that I tried after actual journalistic employment — I knew my own limitations too well for that,— but I began to send round little articles and one or two of them were accepted and I can't tell you how proud I was. Proud, I mean, to see that I was still capable of learning and that within a year or two I might expect to be able to speak President's English quite passably. It is something, after all, to be able to write in two languages and all the more so when they have so many queer surface resemblances. The Germans are very capable linguists; yet you will never find a German who can speak Dutch; it is too much like his own language.

There are several shibboleths by which the

true New Yorker may recognise the provincial young man from England. Here follow four of the most important, by a careful observance of which the Englishman may for a long time escape conviction, even in the Anglo-Saxon metropolis itself. *Imprimis,* he has a fatal habit of using such phrases as "You must," "You should," "It is essential that you —" and so forth, when there is only one safe way of expressing the same idea, "You gotta." Again, he will say, or write — which is even worse —"A quarter to ten." He should say, "A quarter of ten." He will talk of being "called after So-and-so." It should be "named for So-and-so." Finally, he will say "Yes" or "No"— words perfectly unfamiliar to the cultured Anglo-Saxon, who has no real words expressing such ideas. Occasionally, the glosses "Yup" and "Nop" are heard, it is true, though seldom in really cultured circles. I pass over such minor errors as "biscuit" for "crackers" and "ill" for "sick," because even in England the best people are beginning to realise the folly of such insularities.

If you go farther and wish to be accepted not only as American, but as one of the rarest creatures on God's green earth, a native-born New Yorker, you must remember yet one thing more, always to pronounce "th" as "d." If you wish to say that you were looking for three thousand Thespian thieves in Third Avenue, you must say that you were watching out for dree dousand Despian dieves — only you would not say thieves at all, but politicians or State Senators, or smart business men, or something like that. You would say "on Third Avenue," by the way, and never "in." I suppose this curious treatment of the "th" comes from the enormous number of German immigrants in New York, just as does the word "boob," meaning — well, all sorts of things. "He is some boob," for instance, means that he fancies himself quite considerably. There is nothing guttural about the "th"; it is a pure, clean "d," and very characteristic.

To become a graduate in American slang is of the simplest. I think I may say without boasting that I was for a time emeritus professor in the Macgregor University of Eighth Avenue. I picked up an old copy — I think it was in the Bohn edition — of the Vision of Piers Plowman — at a second-hand book-store on Forty-second Street and quoted at random. You will also find much useful information in Roger Occam, while I understand, though I can speak only from hearsay, that the Anglo-Saxon Chronicle is a very mine of up-to-the-hour Americanisms.

I fear that I am wandering somewhat from the path of my vagabondage, but so I actually did in real life when I tended bar for Mr. Macgregor. I occupied, so to put it, a place of profit under Government, a hillock of ease whereon to rest and look back over the devious wanderings of the past few months. Mine again was a position analogous to that of a policeman on point duty outside Charing Cross Station, in that at least a very large section of New York passed daily under my survey. Especially, of course, I was interested in the Englishmen among our patrons. The number of Englishmen in New York is really surprising.

It is pathetic, too, when you come to realise how many of them have drifted there, after failing elsewhere, with some vague hope that it is an Eldorado where they can repair their damaged fortunes. We have been told, *ad nauseam,* that the Americans hate, despise, envy, contemn the English. This and similar statements are absolutely untrue, so far at least as my experience goes, but if it were so it would scarcely be surprising so far as New York is concerned, seeing how large a proportion of the Englishmen seen there are " unemployables "— at either end of the social scale. The capable Englishman goes West; if he stays in New York, where there is really no room for him, he is not capable. I stayed in New York, myself, so I know.

If the New Yorker — and especially the lower class New Yorker — does not hate England and the English, it is not for want of encouragement. The reason is curious enough and has very little to do with Irish Nationalist sentiment, though that of course helps. But it is chiefly a matter of business.

New York has notoriously its gutter press — not more guttery though than is its counterpart in England. It devotes itself to supplying strong meats for the baser part of the populace. They are for the most part Finns, Wallachs, Lithuanians, and a hundred other weird peoples whose very names are scarcely known to us except in fits of depression. The papers who pander to them are forced to attack England, if they would gain their pennies, for two reasons, both unexpected. In the first place patriotism pays, in America as elsewhere, perhaps even a little more; and it is the patriotic duty of every American paper to uphold the banner of America against all comers — as one can only wish were also the case in England. Now, a very good way of praising your own country is to compare it favourably with its foreign sisters. You could not gain any national kudos by pointing out American superiority over Moldo-Wallachia or Crim Tartary; you would only be insulting America by condescending to such a comparison. You must select a more or less worthy rival to give your words some weight. England is the one country in the world which America regards as a worthy rival. Therefore, when the gutter press upholds America at the expense of the outer world, England has to bear the brunt of it. Thus the foreign-born American is gradually being educated to believe that England comprises within herself every national quality which compares unfavourably with her transatlantic daughter. The native-born American does not think so for a moment; with very few exceptions he admires England and likes the English, but he has other things to do than to spend his time protesting that liking.

Another reason which tends towards gutter-abuse of England is the race-war, which has already broken out in the United States and which in a very few years, unless wisely dealt with, may produce serious results. Perhaps less in New York than elsewhere, but very perceptible there also, is the striking fact that all the men of action have English, or more strictly British, names. The financier or the capitalist is very often, though not invariably,

German or Jewish. But the director, the foreman, the manager, the supervisor who comes into personal contact with the working-class, is in the vast majority of cases of British descent. The working-class, which is largely recruited from the weird under-nations already referred to, does not consider itself well-treated. Personally I quite agree with it, though I need not go into that. Whether or no, the man upon whose shoulders it places the responsibility for its sufferings is that representative of the ruling caste with whom it is brought into personal contact — the man of British descent. *Ex pede Herculem.*

At the upper end of the social scale there is certainly little anti-British prejudice. On the contrary, the one indispensable condition of social success is to have a British name. Armed with that you have always the chance of being recognised as an F.F.V., which is to say, the scion of one of the first families of Virginia, which is to say, a descendant of Cavaliers and an acceptable candidate for membership in the Thames Valley Legitimist League or the White

Rose Society or other combination of Die-Hard Jacobites. Failing that, your ancestors came over in the *Mayflower,* which, as has now been proved by the researches of the Smithsonian Institute, was a vessel of about double the size of the *Imperator,* and crowded at that. If you are unlucky enough not to have an English name — but your son always has, so we need not go into that. For some curious reason, it is better to have had an English great-grandfather than an English father. If, I mean, your father was born in Putney, you conceal it, or pretend that it was not Putney, England, but Putney, Massachusetts. If it was your grandfather, you regard Massachusetts or Surrey with equal equanimity. But if it was your great-grandfather — then there is no holding you; you subscribe on the slightest encouragement, or none at all, to funds for the restoration of Putney Parish Church, and if you have not had eighteen generations of crusading ancestors buried there before your fiftieth birthday you are no true American.

My coloured cousin Euphemia was a sufficiently good example of the spiritual empire wielded by England in another direction. I came across one still more suggestive in the days when I was trying to be a journalist. He was an Englishman named Ah Wong Li.

I had been sent to Chinatown, which is the place where the Chinese live, to get up, if I could, a picturesque story concerning a shooting affair which had just taken place there. One of the best assets of the New York paper is the Tong. No New York paper ever gives any more news than it can help about anything that happens outside New York. If the German Emperor, the Tsar, and the French President murdered each other after a drinking bout, the most enterprising New York daily would give the affair three lines, tucked away under an account of how little Flossie Yammerheim, of Avenue A', had won a cooking prize at school, developed into three columns by the help of interviews with her teacher, the local Rabbi, and the delicatessen storekeeper who provided the materials. The next most enterprising journal would give the Yuropian holocaust one line; the rest would not refer to it at all. The New York public cares only for what happens in New York, and, of course, in Mayfair, which is, however, no more than a suburb of Manhattan. Now the Tong — which is a Chinese Secret Society — is New Yorkian and Oriental and picturesque all at the same time. And it is always killing itself or its rivals, which renders it even more eligible. So I was sent to Mott Street to get the details of an affair in which seven Chinamen shot each other dead in a laundry, and five were wounded. And there I met Ah Wong Li. He was the secretary of a flourishing co-operative murder society, and he was very English indeed. He had been educated in Berkshire — he was born in Hong Kong — and he had a contempt for any one not born under the British flag that was quite colossal. The thing that interested him most, apart from the restaurant which he owned, was Imperial Federation. I shall never forget the

I was sent to Mott Street to get the details of an affair.

contempt with which he spoke to another Englishman of Chinese descent, who, however, was only brought to Hong Kong at the age of two, having been born, by an oversight, somewhere in Mongolia.

CHAPTER XVII

Under the Red Light

THERE are only three people in New York who do not profess themselves able to give you full and authentic inside knowledge of the genesis of all police scandals, present, past, and to come. They are all high police officials, and I am not one of them. I really did get some little insight into the "Red Light" system at first hand when, for a time, I acted as assistant doorkeeper at a gambling-hell in the West Forties. That was after I had left Macgregor's saloon, when my vaudeville venture had failed lamentably, and while I was still trying to be a journalist.

It was a regular customer at the café who first induced me to tempt fortune in vaudeville. He was an American — one of the few I ever saw in New York — which meant, of course, that he had a scheme for cornering the whole vaudeville business in the United States, Great Britain being regarded as one of the minor territories. He worked it out down to its smallest details at late sittings in the Family Department, and I have no doubt that it would have turned out a marvellous success if he had been able to raise the five dollars necessary for procuring properly stamped notepaper — an essential preliminary to commercial success in America. I did not regret my temporary connection with him, because it threw me into fortuitous contact with a man who really did manage one of the minor halls on the East Side, and under his auspices I made my first appearance in vaudeville. It only lasted for a week, and I cannot say that it had any very pronounced success, but it was quite good fun while it lasted. I worked the turn with Miss Lamartine, whose name you may remember. She is extremely small; I have been called stout by my enemies, and am rather on the tall side. I was dressed as a baby in long clothes, and Miss Lamartine, attired as the vaudevillists' idea of a nursemaid, pushed me on to the stage in the American apology for a perambulator, and we sang songs and spouted patter and that sort of thing. I think we enjoyed it more than the audience did, because, being mostly Greeks and Italians and Russian Jews, I doubt if they understood what we said; but they were very nice about it, and there were no riots or anything unpleasant. We were not able to get any re-engagements, though, so the speculation came to an end. I can't say that I learned very much about the American music-hall stage in the time; the only difference I could see was that, while in England you do not call your fellow-artists by their Christian names until you have exchanged at least three words, in America you address even your business letters to people you have never seen with some endearing diminutive, and close with love and innumerable kisses.

I had been wise enough not to drop my small journalistic connection in the meantime, but all the same I began looking for another job at once. The free-lance has, if possible, a worse time in New York than in London, so far as getting paid goes. In London, of course, they often make you wait six weeks for your money, putting the responsibility for your meals in the meantime on the broad shoulders of the C.O.S. In New York it frequently runs to three months — or did in my case — and the better class the paper the longer you have to wait. I did some articles for what is generally considered the best daily in New York. After nine weeks I asked for the money. The man I asked was quite annoyed about it, and said I ought to know better than to worry them about such little things. I tried hard for another three weeks, and then was told they could not trace the transaction at all. In the end I got the money by going up to the proprietor's room on the twenty-third floor, sitting on the threshold and moaning through the keyhole. He said it got on his nerves, after two hours, and gave me an order on the cashier. I have never had to do that, even in Carteret — I mean in London.

It was through my journalism that I became a gambling-hell official. I wanted to make myself favourably known in other ways than by emulating Lazarus. I went to my old patron Officer Dempsey and asked for suggestions, and he got me the job. It was in a plain brown freestone house in one of the semi-residential streets between Sixth Avenue and Broadway. Most of the gaming places and disorderly houses and all-night sing-songs are clustered about there, along with theatrical lodging houses and cheap restaurants — a sort of New York Shaftesbury Avenue, in fact. Ours was a very discreet establishment with lace curtains in the windows, and a high flight of steps running up to the front door. It was owned by an alderman, and the upper part was let out in lodgings to theatre people. We occupied only the basement and the ground floor. Like other lawless places in New York it was run on lines of almost monastic respectability, voices scarcely raised above a whisper until pretty early in the morning, drunken men put comfortably to bed on sofas in an ante-room, and that sort of thing. We had a higher-class connection than most of our rivals, and for rather a curious reason; the police on duty never directed any chance customers our way, everything was done by introduction. In the ordinary way, when you feel like gambling or otherwise amusing yourself disreputably in New York you make for that section of Broadway between the corner of Central Park — Fifty-ninth Street if I remember aright — and Macey's — popularly known as the "Great White Way," because of its electric flashlight advertisements — and ask the first policeman you come across where to go, and he gives you a list of addresses. You can ask a taxi-driver, if you prefer it, but the establishments he recommends are not usually of the first-class.

Now the reason that my particular hell was not recommended by the police was that it was not officially a gambling house at all. The alderman and other highly placed gentlemen who own the Vice Trust have, of course, reduced it to a very exact business, of which each branch keeps strictly to its own affairs. Thus an alderman who runs gambling-hells is not supposed to dabble in disorderly houses; if he does, it must be secretly and at the risk of being raided by the police, as not paying the appropriate rates of blackmail. Our proprietor nominally confined his activities to the White Slave side of the business, in which he was what you might call the managing director. But he was of a Napoleonic turn of mind, and yearned also after the profits — reported to be higher — of the gambling side. Hence we were nominally a disorderly house and as such described in the official records — and only paid that scale of blackmail, the lower of the two. Consequently we were extremely discreet and well-managed. In that particular block you might, every night regularly, Sundays included, hear the strains of "Everybody's Doing It" wafted to heaven from innumerable gramophones, from midnight to nine or ten next morning; you might hear drunken choruses, feminine screams of "Murder," and other sounds of gaiety, at all hours. But never from our house. We might have been a community of bishops for any sign to the contrary.

We were not raided while I was there, and

there were no disturbances of any kind. The life, in fact, was deadly dull, although the pay was good; and I learnt how to play quite a number of games hitherto unknown to me. But the champagne was execrable — some abominable Californian brand put up in Perrier Jouet bottles — and I was afraid of diabetes and left.

CHAPTER XVIII

In the Matter of Manners

THERE are many Englishmen — some of whom have been there — who quite conscientiously maintain that the street-manners of New York are the worst prevailing in any great city. There are a number of New Yorkers who will tell you, equally conscientiously, the same of London. So Paris sneers at Berlin and Berlin at Paris, and I suppose Pekin at Tokio and vice-versa. What is more they are all perfectly correct according to their lights. London points with pride to the theatre-queue; Berlin rejoices in the feline smile with which its inhabitants remove their hats on entering a shop; Paris will say and truly that its most uncultured Apache takes off a victim with a grace unknown in brutaller climes; New York might claim, if it liked —

though it is too busy abusing him for things that he can't help — that the manner of Officer Dempsey towards a harassed foreigner is the kindliest form of courtesy anywhere to be found. The Parisian does not barge his way into a tram-car on a wet day — because a kindly administration provides him with a duly numbered ticket — but watch him on the outskirts of a crowd when he wants to see the centre of interest. The Englishman will cold-shoulder his railway companion, boorishly, because he is shy and self-conscious; the American will lean across the aisle and speculate upon the price you have paid for your overcoat, because he really takes a friendly interest in you. Each of them will think the other appallingly rude, and each will be quite right and very wrong.

I am acknowledged, in England, to have really charming manners. I say this, not in any spirit of petty pride, but because it illustrates my point. A New York acquaintance, long since become a friend, has assured me that when I was first introduced to him, at his club, he disliked me cordially, setting me down as prig, oaf, boor and I know not what beside. When I asked him upon what he had based this unfavourable verdict he replied: "Because, from your manner, I thought you must be God's first cousin." Passing over the fact that such a Personage would probably have excellent manners, that I laid no claim to such relationship and that I never met an Englishman who did, except he imply it in the well-founded belief that English is the only language spoken in heaven, I will only say that at the time I was doing my very best to make a favourable impression. I am not, of course, by a very long way, the only Englishman who has unwittingly gained for himself a similar reputation in New York. In my case, as it fortunately or unfortunately happened, the Fates busied themselves to impress upon me that so far from being a demigod I was no more than the humblest vagabond that creeps the earth. Many Englishmen never have this brought to their notice and they go through the world, quite unaware of the claim they appear to be making to divine honours — and so create for all their countrymen an uncomplimentary legend that sticks.

The Englishman usually considers New York a home of incivility because he is socially and psychologically out of his element. He expects, from those whom at home he is accustomed to consider his inferiors, a degree of deference to which no American — however humble his status — would admit his right. If he would only regard the policeman, the tram-conductor, the railway guard as a man and a brother, he would find them individually charming. But he judges them by their uniforms and expects from them the deference paid by a private in parade kit to a subaltern in mufti. Contrariwise, the American in England discovers in people of those same occupations a manner which strikes him as subservient, servile, even cringing. It is not so in reality, because it is only a uniform, put on for the moment in deference to custom, but acknowledged by all parties to be no more than a uniform. The footman in livery who should find himself treated as a man and a brother by some American guest at his master's house would consider himself, and very properly, insulted. One does not speak to the man at the wheel; and he is for the time at the wheel, guiding the social ship along its appointed track. Once in plain clothes and the case is altered; he will hob-nob with you and treat you well as a free Englishman should and does treat the stranger within his gates — and uncommonly good company you will find him.

Broadly speaking you will never decide whether the American or the Englishman, the Parisian or the Berliner or the Cypriote or the Tibetan, is the best-mannered until you can establish a fixed basis of absolute value which will cover soap and beer and creamcheese and moonlight and poetry and prose. But it is possible to establish an internal standard in each and all. So far as it is possible for an outsider to gauge the matter the New Yorker would have no reputation for bad manners anywhere in the world, for his scale, being based upon the common humanity of human beings, is a high one, were it not that he rejoices — really rejoices — in one particular sect or creed or religion who make it their business in life to cultivate bad manners to their logical conclusion. I refer, of course, as anyone who has ever lived in New York will know already — to the men who work the elevators in the big public buildings.

As I was, after abandoning my employment in the gambling world, for a time a member of that profession I can speak with some authority. I do not think any other trade or profession in the world could seriously challenge the supremacy of the New York elevator-attendant. I know, of course, that the young duchesses employed in those "lunch" establishments which correspond to our tea-shops deserve honourable mention. They are very rude indeed and haughty — a shade more so I think than the staff of a temperance hotel in England — but they are, after all, young women, and of a class from which one expects little courtesy, unless one is a nut, dude, or buck. Also they may be put to shame; which certainly can be said of no liftman anywhere in the Union. I saw a neat rout of this kind in one of Child's lunch places — popularly known as the "Café des Enfants"— near Times Square. A Frenchman, obviously a new importation, was paying his bill at the cash desk. The girl flung him a nickel change, so carelessly that it rolled back, through the little grille to a place under her elbow where it was almost impossible to retrieve it from without. The Frenchman waited for her to hand it back to him, but she only regarded him with the air of bovine offensiveness which is the trade-mark of her sex and class throughout the world. I have often wondered why this should be so, why, I mean, the young woman employed in a post-office or a telephone exchange or a teashop, or a temperance hotel — though not in a public-house, where I suppose the softening influence of alcoholic association makes her more genial — should be so ubiquitously offensive to everyone who is not her personal friend of the other sex. Is it that she believes it "ladylike?" Or that she knows herself for the poor defenceless little creature that she is and like a gecko lizard assumes for defence the guise of a ravaging dragon. Is it — but I am wandering from the point.

The Frenchman, then, waited for a while and at last, removing his hat, bowed and smiled affably. "You may keep it, my good girl," he said, "as the reward of your politeness." I was next to him in the queue of filled customers waiting to pay, and it pleased me greatly to watch the young woman grow purple to the ears and hand across the nickel without a word. An elevator-man would not have been confused. He would have pocketed the coin and cursed the Frenchman because it was not more. I am inclined to think that, by some secret Trade Union regulation, elevator-attendants always marry young ladies employed in tea-shops, and that the daughters always follow the mother's profession, while the sons become either liftmen or hotel bell-boys. I do not know whether this is actually the case, because while I was an elevator attendant I never happened to be on intimate terms with a "lunch" waitress, nor do I know if it is peculiar to New York or also in operation in London. I shall find out in time. It is such speculations as these that make the vagabond's life interesting if not lucrative.

If, as I suppose, hotel bell-boys, promoted on attaining maturity to hotel-clerkships, are actually the offspring of liftmen — (It is curious by the way how "hustling" America always prefers the longer of two words while lazy, effete England selects the shorter) — and of tea-shop girls, they are in some degree an example of atavism. Bell-boy, hotel-clerk and, to a lesser degree, waiter, are all alike tainted with the un-American vice of servility and must, therefore, granted the correctness of my suggested pedigree, throw back to some remote European forebear — perhaps the warder of a feudal castle. They are insolent only intermittently; before the guest of proven wealth they grovel with a subservience elsewhere unknown. The elevator-man, on the other hand, is insolent to rich and poor alike, to the millionaire as to the clerk, to the pretty girl as to the faded female with six parcels and a string bag. It is with him a cult, a duty, a religion. I believe — I do not know, for I was never admitted to the inner mysteries of the profession — that there is some hidden God of Insolence to whom he offers incense before going on duty, as did the devotees of Thuggism to the red goddess Kali. There is something very admirable in this fidelity to an ideal — seen from a distance of seven thousand miles or so. Unfortunately, here and there is to be found a traitor. Four several times in my experience have I come across an elevator-attendant approximating in manners and deportments to the ordinary human being outside the Mysteries. It is true that, without exception, they were only coloured men.

It was by the merest chance that I became a deputy-elevator man. After I left my Tenderloin job I wandered down to Macgregor's saloon to see if there was anything going, and there I met with Mr. Mooney. It is a curious detail, by the way, that I never met an elevator-man who was not of pure

British descent, except of course the coloured men, and even they were Barbadians. Upon the events, simple as they were, of that one evening, I might base a whole essay upon the advantages of America over any European country you care to mention as a place of residence when you are out of work and honestly looking for it. I was not inside the saloon for more than half-an-hour, yet within that time I had two spontaneous offers of employment, both offering at least a living wage. I wonder how many public-houses you might enter, say in Southwark, before you received even one. Yet New York is generally said by the rest, and especially the West of the continent, to be the grave of hopes, so far as making a living is concerned and a poor man in question.

The first offer came from a " boy " employed by the Western Union Telegraph Company. I call him a boy, because so he called himself, though he was at least sixty-five, very grizzled and inextricably wrinkled. I foregathered with him several times previously and we found a common interest in, of all things in the world, superstition and the history of witchcraft. I once wrote a very clever book about it — it is still on sale, I have no doubt, if anyone cares to buy it. Denier, as my boyish friend was called, had thought about it — more deeply, I fear, than ever I did — and so we became friends. That is another unexpected side to New York. Imagine dropping into the public bar of the "King's Arms" in Lower Sloane Street and meeting there a casual labourer interested in the Cabbala and the Rosy Cross.

Denier's offer was that of dog-leader. A wealthy lady of Madison Avenue had four dogs who suffered from indigestion through lack of exercise. Their former attendant had been dismissed at short notice, having contracted a cold in the head and a habit of sniffing, which was bad for the nerves of his charges. The hours were few, the occupation light — no more than strolling in Central Park, — and the pay good. I was not starving at the moment, though, and so I declined and two minutes later I was introduced to Mr. Mooney.

Mr. Mooney was what I may describe as the

Deputy-Assistant-Adjutant-General of the elevator service in a huge Broadway building that had eight sets of lifts running at once. He was a small person, with a game leg and an expression of determined malevolence that was purely professional. Naturally he was very amiable, as I found when he gave up at least an hour to explaining to me the details of my duty, though it was not at all his own to do so. One of his subordinates was laid up with a sudden chill, and he was watching out for a substitute; and I happened to come along at the right moment, and Mr. Macgregor vouched for me and I was engaged on the spot.

I had no idea at first of my own good fortune. There is, the poet has told us, no greater happiness than is provided by satisfied hatred. I was to experience it. The building over whose lifts Mr. Mooney reigned, with a crooked ash-stick for sceptre (about which he had a marvellous tale to tell, including two murders and an heroic rescue) — housed the offices of a great daily paper with which I had been connected at the time of my first arrival in America and against whose money editor, city editor and editor-in-chief I had three separate and distinct grudges. Let me here remark upon one peculiarity of newspaper life in America. A newspaper staff consists entirely of editors. From the smallest boy who carries messages, up through all the grades which we should know as compositors and proof-readers and reporters and sub-editors and managers, in America there are none but editors. They start at the top with about twelve editors-in-chief and work down to a regiment of editresses corresponding to charwomen in London, but transatlantically known as scrub-lady editresses. When I was working express elevator No. 6 I became, without knowing it, an editor — assistant-express-elevator-editor I think it was officially called — from the fifteenth to the twenty-third floors, on which the newspaper offices were situated. Below them I lapsed, as it were, into private life again.

If satisfied revenge is the highest human happiness I certainly attained it in that editorial post. Being the express, which was to say the fastest running of the elevators, it was that most used by my fellow-editors. On the very first day I carried upwards, in one load, my three old-time enemies. By a still more remarkable coincidence that elevator broke down between the sixth and seventh floors and stuck there. It stuck for something like twenty minutes, and all that time I was in the happy position of an Early Christian lion surrounded by martyrs. I had them all on their knees, and two of them in tears, before I let them out.

I did not keep that post very long — having been appointed only as a stop-gap — but I think I can honestly say that I did nothing to lower the high standard of the profession in the way of ill-manners. It was curious how natural they became and how soon. On my first day I several times as nearly as possible disgraced myself for good and all. An old gentleman, I remember, who was carrying a number of parcels, dropped one, and I picked it up and handed it to him. Fortunately none of my colleagues saw me — it happened on the entrance floor; but I still remember the flush of shame that came over me at the thought of how I had betrayed them. Twenty-four hours later an old lady slipped as she entered and nearly fell. I felt the impulse to go to her assistance, but mastered it in time. By the third day if all the old ladies in Manhattan had fallen round me in sheafs and been in imminent danger I should have jeered at them with absolute spontaneity.

Why this should be I have never been able to decide — the inevitable rudeness of the New York liftman, I mean. A policeman has as much power — yet he is always amiable; a bar-tender is as much respected — yet he is the essence of politeness. I believed for a time that electricity might have something to do with it, yet the hydraulic liftman is as rude as any of his fellows. Only one clue I have discovered. Those in charge of express elevators are, speaking generally, ruder than their "calling at every floor" brethren. Possibly the rush of blood to the head — and feet — consequent upon continual careering up and down at great speed may have something to do with it. Some day I am going to study the English liftman and his manners, and perhaps, with his help, evolve a theory.

As I say, my experience was but short, yet it will always be a satisfaction to remember that I was for a time a member of a caste quite superior to the ordinary decencies of life, and one which, rightly or wrongly, has been enabled to erect its personal and trade idiosyncrasy into an international legend.

CHAPTER XIX

"Follow the Crowd"

WHILE I was in New York the gentleman ubiquitously known — and loved in some places — as " Boss Croker," happened to return from Europe where, for some reason best known to himself, he now elects to live. He was, of course, welcomed by many reporters and to them he loosed one gem of thought, which I have ever since remembered. It was that he thanked God he had again returned to a city conducted on modern and progressive lines.

Of course Mr. Croker is a better judge of municipal management than I could ever hope to be. I have been told that he has freely expended his life and his intelligence and his large private fortune on the furtherance of purity and the stamping out of " graft " and similar abuses in municipal life. I had intended therefore to refer to him as a typical American citizen, had not another American citizen, who is my very good friend, practically threatened me with personal violence if I did anything of the sort.

As a mere outsider and looker-on I do not profess to understand the rights of this. I will therefore only say that, while I do not altogether agree with the anti-European innuendo contained in the Great Thought I have quoted, I am thoroughly in agreement with what Mr. Croker went on to say: That New York beyond all other cities exemplifies the progress of democracy. In so far as the aim and end of democracy is to exalt the crowd above the individual, New York can certainly give points even to Glasgow, with Manchester a bad third and London altogether out of the running.

I am not, for my sins, a believer in democracy. My own little preference in the way of government, if I had any voice in the matter, which thank God I never had, would be for a benevolent despotism tempered by assassination. I believe, I mean, that it is better for ten thousand ciphers to die if thereby One Man may be brought to perfect fruition. But in this I know that I am very silly, even impious, and that when I get to the next world it will be proved to me, painfully. Be that as it may, New York is to me the most interesting of the modern cities with which I have any personal acquaintance because it does, more than any of its sister-capitals, exemplify that side of democracy which entails, not all for one, but one for all.

We laugh, in London loudly, in New York more discreetly — by "we" I mean the people who make their living out of the public by pandering to its preferences — at the "rubberer," *anglice* the man whose neck, through constant straining to see over the heads of the crowd, has become elastic. Yet he typifies the whole community, as, in the future, I suppose, the whole democratic world. I can speak with authority, because I was for a time one of the objects of his most earnest regard.

That is to say that after I left my post as deputy-assistant-express-elevator-editor, I sat for three weeks in the window of a shop on Broadway illustrating the virtues of a razor strop. It was really a very good razor strop, though after a time I became prejudiced against it; but I chiefly remember it now as connected with innumerable round pink things, like anemones in an aquarium, all pressing against the outside of the glass, and innumerable solemn eyes staring at me like cows. They used to fascinate me so much that I forgot altogether I was supposed to be cutting shavings off blocks of wood with the razors I had sharpened, and just stared back at them. Not that that reduced the crowds; once started they would have gone on staring just the same if a black cloth had been drawn right across the shop front. I won a dollar from a guileless New Yorker over that once by a trick very, very old in London, but of course new to New York. I bet him that I could draw a crowd of a thousand people in ten minutes by merely standing still. I did it, with minutes to spare, by staring at the corner of a tailor's window. I forget whether three or four men were clubbed to death before the police could clear the sidewalk — four, I think.

If a London tailor wants to advertise the excellence of his wares he endeavours to intimate that they are intended only for the select few. If he is in New York he sets about it like this: "Seven million smart young chaps are wearing our Ten-Dollar, Ready-to-Wear, Tuxedo Suitings. Follow the Crowd." They do, too. No true New Yorker would think of putting on a pair of trousers until he was quite sure that at least a million others had preceded him in them. In my window, just over my head, was a large ticket, setting forth how many millions of my razor strop had been sold. One of my duties was to be handed a telegram every half-hour, to open it with an expression of wonder, and to add another half-million to the total above me. We began with a million and a-quarter, I remember, and I put my foot in it rather badly. It was a new line, only put on the market that morning, and I suggested that it would be just as well to start with a really impressive number — ten or twenty million. The shop-manager was very much annoyed. He said that the proprietor was the head of I forget what religious community, and had all his life long set his face against business trickery and exaggerations, and that if I wanted to deceive the public I had better go elsewhere to do it. I did after a bit, because there was another store, two blocks down, where they wanted a man to recline in a newly invented chair and do nothing except read a novel, with a little nigger boy to change the totals for him, and that struck me as better suited to my capacities. I had to wait, though, for a time, because there was a lot of competition for the post, and meanwhile I got corns all over my palms from the razor handles. All the same, I was sorry I had changed afterwards, when I found I was expected to read the same novel over and over again, to save wear and tear. It was by Mrs. Humphrey Ward, and I learned it by heart and used to recite it to myself at night, and I think

I should have gone mad if I had not been struck by a bright idea. I suggested to the manager that it would go down well with the religious public if I were to read something of an improving tendency, and he thought well of it and got a second-hand Old Testament cheap — which would appeal, he said, to Jews and Christians alike — and I learned that by heart, too, which proved extremely useful later on, when I received a call to the ministry — but that is a purely private matter.

I was first struck by the sameness of the democratic crowd on noticing one day that all the men who were staring at me were wearing coats of exactly the same cut and colour, and had their lips pursed into exactly the same lines, and their hair shaved away behind their ears to exactly the same width, and wore their hats at exactly the same angle and bent their heads over their left shoulders — never the right — in exactly the same way. After that I studied the matter more closely, and it never varied. If one man wore an overcoat they all did, and if one man was smoking a particular kind of cigar they all did — and it was just the same with the women. It puzzled me for a time, because I did not realise how they were able to time the changes so exactly. I found out at last that it was through reading the newspapers. There was one really terrible spring day when half the men I saw were wearing straw hats and the other half black billycocks. There was a dreadful look of uncertainty on their faces, too, and from the side-long way they kept looking at each other instead of at me, I was afraid there was going to be a revolution or something. What had really happened was that the *Evening Journal* and the *Telegram* had fallen out over whether Straw-Hat day ought to fall on the Wednesday or the Thursday. It had something to do with the Gregorian Calendar, I think, and the Equinoxes, but the result was quite dreadful. I forget how many suicides were attributed to that dispute, owing to the prevalent uncertainty, but on the Thursday, when both authorities were united in saying that the day had really come when straw hats were *de rigueur* the sigh of relief that went up throughout the City — and the State, too, I expect — made Broadway sound like the inside of a volcano.

The real reason for all this is the fierce desire to be American. If you remember that of the whole population of New York only three individuals are officially recorded to have been born in America at all, that two of them died in infancy and the third was electrocuted, you will realise that this ideal is not so easy of achievement as it looks, or would not be but for the newspapers and the advertising tailors. Thanks to them, though, every native-born New Yorker as soon as he arrives from Cracow, Odessa, or Lozengrad, as the case may be, no sooner lands than he is seized upon by his relatives — or if he have none, by the Immigration officers — and inducted into the regulation suit, hat, cut of hair, smile, or frown, whichever is for the moment most American — and so passes at once into the indistinguishable ruck. Within three weeks he has learned to think, within a month to speak, in precisely the same way as do the rest of his fellow citizens, and within a year he was born in Jersey City and his great-great-grandfather came from England. That is one reason why if you make a hit in America it is such a very big hit indeed. If one man admires a book, or a play, or a rag-time melody, or a new brand of Frankfurters or religion, the whole population does so unanimously — and contrariwise. It is the same in politics and patriotism and morals generally. "Follow the crowd," says the native-born New Yorker, "and you can't go wrong."

As the loyal subject of a Monarch, with an Established Church, for the moment at any rate, a titled aristocracy and a catechism which reminds me of my duty towards my betters, I might be inclined to sneer at this, were it not that England also to-day exalts Demos to a seat among the gods. If we are ready to admit — which I for one am not — that Jack is as good as his master and better, too — then there can be no question that Mr. Croker has the rights of it. We are all going the same way and New York is going a little faster than London — and Pekin, if all accounts be true —

faster than either. Let us then, and all together, do our little best to hasten the day when, throughout all the world, we shall all change felt for straw upon Straw-Hat day. Only let us, wherever we may be, see to it that someone does not make handsome profit out of our fidelity to an impossible ideal — as it may be is the case to-day in New York and nearer home.

CHAPTER XX

Eastward Ho!

EXPERIENCE is, I have no doubt, very useful in the art of steam-ship stoking if you propose to adopt it as your permanent profession; which you do not, except as an alternative to a life sentence or the electric chair. If you approach it only as an amateur, you can get along without any very great skill. You need a lot of strength in your arms, though, and a sound heart, lungs and other incidentals. If you are predisposed to bad colds in the head, you will find it healthier to commit a murder, after all.

Nevertheless, a stoker, so far as my personal experience goes, has many advantages. For one thing, he does not have to wash. He may if he wishes to, of course — I never heard of any regulation against it — but as nothing short of flaying would make any difference, he does not usually worry about it. Similarly, he does not have to think about clothes. He generally wears an eyeglass and a smile, or something like that, unless he is very proud of his figure, which I personally am not, but they are at best a vanity. Lastly, he is treated by his superior officers, captains, pursers, engineers and the like, as though he were a duke. I know that such is not the popular impression, but I speak from personal knowledge. It is true that when I assisted to work a certain Atlantic liner that shall be nameless eastward from New York, I was one of a happy family of what are known in American labour circles as "scabs" or in England as blacklegs.

It was by accident rather than design that I became a stoker and a scab. I was doing fairly well in New York at the time, which is to say that I quite frequently had enough to eat. What is more I had excellent prospects. More fortunate even than the proverbial ass I had three distinct avenues of occupation open before me. I had the chance — yes, really —

of entering the ministry. It came from Connecticut, through my old friend Mr. Wolff, who wrote that he believed me to have hidden somewhere deep within me the means of grace; and that two of the bears were dead, and that a third had got into trouble through trying to embrace the wife of a leading member of the flock. Then through a chance meeting with Cap Lane, who was on his way to get married, I heard that Helga's father had made a standing offer to give me employment in his business, which had something to do with typewriting. I learnt from Cap Lane, by the way, that Helga herself had assured him that I was a Russian Prince fleeing from the displeasure of my uncle the Tsar, so it was clear to me that her health had not suffered from immersion. My friend Dempsey was back on his beat again and when I told him how I had been mistaken for a detective at Amicus, he suggested that, granted a sufficient "pull," towards which he thought he might himself assist me, I might enter the police-force with good prospects of becoming a "sleuth" in actual fact.

My prospects were thus at their brightest at the moment I left New York, though only as I hope temporarily. Unable to decide between the various dazzling prospects opening out before me, I temporised. They were expecting a strike on at one of the big hotels Central Park way. There usually is of course an hotel strike on hand in New York, but I happened to hear of this through a man I met at Macgregor's. They expected to want temporary waiters for a week or two and it occurred to me that I wanted a dress suit. The strike was not to be declared for a fortnight or so, and while the New York tailors obstinately refused to give me credit I knew there was one in London upon whose infinite credulity I thought I could still build. I calculated I should just have time to see London again, get some clothes and be back in time to report for work.

Just then, by some oversight, one of the newspapers paid me some money it owed me, which, with the eighty-five cents I had saved up, made up enough for the return trip, steerage.

That decided me and I went off to book my

passage and just in time I heard of that heaven-sent seamen's strike, and so I got my passage and fifteen dollars as well. Glory be! Incidentally I was fifty times better off as a stoker than were the unhappy steerage passengers who had paid about a pound a day each for the privilege of being bullied.

I suppose there never was such a mixed crowd of stokers since the days of Noah. The authorities of the line were very anxious to get the boat over to England, where there was no strike and they could count on getting a crew, so they took anyone they could get. Many of us had never been to sea before, and as the passage was on the rough side, the scenes in the stoke-hold the first and second days out would require the pen of a lady novelist to do them justice. We took eleven days on the voyage instead of seven, and by the time we reached port most of us were convalescent. I was very popular with my superiors, because I was fool enough not to tumble to the idea of being sea-sick until it was too late, and really did quite a lot of shovelling. It was quite hard work, too, especially when, as frequently happened, the laws of gravity entailed that you should stand on your head every few minutes while the ship made up her mind which way she would dodge a particularly truculent wave. We had been everywhere and done everything from driving a milk-cart to directing a coal trust, everything except stoking, that is to say. A number of us were coloured — naturally — we drew no absurd colour line — and by a curious coincidence the coloured men were all near relations to Booker Washington — all except one, who was in my watch and was of a religious turn of mind. He was eighty-fourth in direct descent from one of the Magi — Balthazar, if I remember aright — and very proud of it.

A " scab " does not expect to be popular, but I am bound to say that never before or since have so many people been anxious to make my acquaintance. They used to hang about outside the company's wharf by fifties at a time, beseeching us for interviews, and holding out half-bricks and paving stones and clubs and revolvers to tempt us with. We were not destined to meet them personally; we were taken aboard by tug, starting from an East River wharf way up on the other side of the island where they did not expect us, and when we got on shipboard we stayed there. They were not discouraged, and when the voyage started they chartered a couple of tugs and accompanied us down the harbour shouting farewells and other things through megaphones. A pleasant little rumour went round about then that we should probably find dynamite bombs in the coal-bunkers, find them after we had fed them into the furnaces and departed skyward, that is to say.

If it has its drawbacks, scabbing has its advantages as well. With the object-lesson of their late employés before them, those in authority bestir themselves to make you happy and comfortable. They don't have to worry about the passengers, because *they* can't strike, or if they did, they would only be playing into the Company's hands, who would put them in irons or something, and feed them on bread and water and save money. They couldn't do that to us, unless they wanted to remain permanently stranded in mid-Atlantic like the Flying Dutchman. We did not waste time either in letting them know exactly how matters stood: those of us I mean who were not sea-sick.

The day after leaving New York the stalwarts among us explained that we really could not work if we were not better fed. We were getting the same food as the steerage passengers at that time, but afterwards we were given second-cabin fare, and what we left was given to the steerage. We got discontented again a day or two later — there were more of us by that time — and the captain, and the chief engineer, and the purser all apologised to us one after the other, and said we could have anything we felt we fancied — and took it out of the unhappy steerage passengers. I never realised before the amazing patience, if that is the right name for it, of the poor. They were mostly Italians from the coal-mining districts of Pennsylvania, who were going back to Italy for a holiday. There was a sprinkling of English, and no Americans. It was an American ship, and they knew better. They were paying very much what they would have to pay at a decent hotel in England, yet they were bullied, and swindled, and abused by every one, from the stewards down to the ship's boys. They slept on mattresses stuffed with some kind of mouldy seaweed. It was one of my jobs to help empty those mattresses overboard after we reached England, and I shall not forget it in a hurry. They had three iron basins without any water to wash themselves in — about a hundred of them — with the result that they didn't wash at all throughout the voyage; such a thing as a bath was undreamt of — except in the advertisements of the line — and the lavatory accommodation would have insulted the dirtiest hog that ever wallowed. Most of the food they got was uneatable, the meat tainted, and so forth. I am not exaggerating when I say that we of the crew refused it. Fortunately for them they were not over-crowded. What it must be like on a West-bound trip, when the boat is crammed from bow to stern, is wonderful to think. This, as I say, was an American boat, but I am told that the conditions are just the same on the English lines; that the French are rather better; and that the Germans do actually treat their steerage passengers as though they were something moderately human. I know that not a day passed but I thanked the kindly Providence that had saved me from such a fate, and made me a free stoker and a gentleman.

It was a pleasant voyage in many ways. For one thing, there was no attempt at discipline, so far as the crew was concerned. About two-thirds of us — stokers, stewards, deck-hands, or whatever our technical names might be — had never been on board ship before. The unhappy officers soon found it was useless to try to teach us anything, so they did the work themselves. The rest of us spent our time grumbling and playing cards and tossing for ha'pence when we were not flirting with the young ladies of the steerage. When we were off duty we spent most of our time with the steerage passengers — which was, of course, strictly forbidden — and a very decent set of people they were, with, as I have said, an infinite capacity of patience. I amused myself trying to get up a conspiracy among them to murder the dispensary steward, whose manners annoyed me, in order to call attention to their grievances, and I think that something might have come of it if one of the men had not possessed a mandolin and another a guitar. Accordingly, instead of murdering and mutinying, they spent their whole time dancing and singing "Funiculi, Funicula." There was, of course, a great preponderance of men, who thus had to dance together, and most beautifully they waltzed. Some of the Anglo-Saxons endeavoured to introduce the Turkey Trot and the Grizzly Bear Hug, but they were frowned upon, I am glad to say.

We reached port in safety at last, more through luck than judgment, I for one believe, and there I drew my money and got into the funny little English toy-train, and raced up to London through the pretty little countryside that looks so neat and clean and sweet that you are kept in agonies all the time lest somebody shall drop a piece of paper out of the train on it and spoil it. It was a weird voyage and I don't know that I particularly want to play at being a scab stoker again. But I did learn one piece of wisdom which was more than worth it. The next time I am very hard up and want to go to America, I shall not go as a steerage passenger; I shall save my money and go as a stowaway. They are quite as well fed and lodged and very much better treated.

THE END

www.ingramcontent.com/pod-product-compliance
Lightning Source LLC
LaVergne TN
LVHW010556110826
845149LV00003B/675

* 9 7 8 1 4 1 8 1 8 7 5 9 0 *